Becoming a
Consultant

Becoming a
Consultant

*How to start and run a profitable
consulting business*

SUSAN NASH

How To Books

First published in 1999 by
How To Books Ltd, 3 Newtec Place,
Magdalen Road, Oxford OX4 1RE, United Kingdom.
Tel: (01865) 793806. Fax: (01865) 248780.
email: info@howtobooks.co.uk
http//www.howtobooks.co.uk

British Library Cataloguing in Publication Data
A catalogue record for this book is available from
the British Library

Cartoons by Mike Flanagan
Cover design by Shireen Nathoo Design
Cover image PhotoDisc

Produced for How To Books by Deer Park Productions
Edited by Julie Nelson
Typeset by PDQ Typesetting, Stoke-on-Trent, Staffs.
Printed and bound by Cromwell Press, Trowbridge, Wiltshire

NOTE: The material contained in this book is set out in good
faith for general guidance and no liability can be accepted
for loss or expense incurred as a result of relying in particular
circumstances on statements made in the book. The laws and
regulations are complex and liable to change, and readers should
check the current position with the relevant authorities before
making personal arrangements.

Contents

List of illustrations 8

Preface 9

1 Defining consulting 11
The business environment in the year 2000 and beyond 11
The shamrock organisation 12
What is consulting? 13
The consulting industry 14
Advantages and disadvantages of working for a consulting
firm 15
Objectives of this book 16
Approach 17

2 Evaluating your fit 18
Advantages and disadvantages of consulting 18
Does consulting suit you? 20
Checklist 29
Case studies 29
Action points 31

3 Getting started and building Key Result Areas 32
Defining your vision 32
Identifying your unique selling proposition 35
SWOT analysis 37
Understanding Key Result Areas 39
Establishing your Key Result Areas 41
Checklist 43
Case studies 43
Action points 47

4 Establishing your business direction 48
Writing a business plan 48
Deciding your legal structure 51

Tax and other financial implications 52
Defining overall goals 54
Setting objectives 54
Establishing milestones 58
Checklist 59
Case studies 60
Action points 62

5 Marketing your business **63**
Creating your marketing plan 63
Using promotional strategies 70
Establishing your network 75
Checklist 77
Case studies 78
Action points 80

6 Selling your service **81**
Overcoming your fear of selling 81
The sales process 82
Establishing sales objectives 85
Telephone marketing 86
Managing the sales meeting 93
Writing successful proposals 97
Using cover letters 101
Formalising contracts 101
Checklist 102
Case studies 103
Action points 105

7 Financing your business **106**
Estimating your start-up costs 106
Finding sources of capital 107
Establishing financial objectives 109
Creating revenue and cash flow statements 110
Setting your billing rate 112
Using different fee arrangements 116
Collecting fees 119
Limiting your exposure to bad debts 120
Charging for sub-contracting 121
Checklist 123
Case studies 123
Action points 125

8 Organising your business   **126**
Setting up your organisation structure   126
Organising your paper flow   131
Planning your activities   133
Establishing organisation/administration objectives   139
Checklist   139
Case studies   140
Action points   141

9 Running your business: doing the work   **142**
Structuring consulting assignments   142
Consulting components   145
Establishing project objectives   148
Checklist   149
Case studies   149
Action points   151

10 Moving into action   **152**
So what will you do now?   152
Checklist   153
Case studies   154
Action points   155

Glossary   156

Appendix: questions for gathering information   159

Further reading   162

Index   163

List of Illustrations

1 The Shamrock Organisation 13
2 Categories for successful consultants 21
3 Consulting process 21
4 Self-assessment – example 27
5 Self-assessment – form 28
6 Strategic planning pyramid 33
7 Conscious/unconscious – competence/incompetence quadrant 36
8 Key Result Areas – example 44
9 Key Result Areas – form 44
10 Key Result Areas and objectives – example 56
11 Key Result Areas and objectives – form 57
12 Establishing milestones – example 59
13 Establishing milestones – form 60
14 Features and benefits of a table 67
15 Features and benefits of a service 68
16 Features and benefits – form 69
17 Promotional activities 71
18 The sales process 82
19 Telephone interaction – person is there and it's a good time 90
20 Telephone interaction – person is there and it's not a good time 91
21 Telephone interaction – person is not there and you get voicemail 92
22. Sales meeting: SELL 98
23 Revenue statement 110
24 Cost statement 111
25 Profit/loss statement 111
26 Cash flow statement 112
27 Planning your activities 133
28 Weekly plan – example 135
29 Weekly plan – form 136
30 Daily plan – form 138

Preface

The business environment is changing drastically. No longer are there long-term employment and job security. Consulting has become a viable and growing working option for individuals in the 1990s and beyond. However, consulting does not provide a miracle solution to work options.

This book has been designed to give you the techniques and a methodology to set up and run your own consulting business. After reading it, you will have a clear understanding of consulting and the entire consulting process. In addition, you will understand the benefits and challenges of consulting as a career choice and learn if your own strengths and challenges fit into the consulting lifestyle. You will be able to define and establish the strategic direction for your consulting business and you will learn skills and practical tools to make your business a reality.

You will understand how to raise finances and maintain financial control of your business, be able to create and implement a marketing strategy and know how to balance on-going business while maintaining the marketing process.

As a result of reading this book you will be able to evaluate whether consulting is an option you wish to consider. If you decide yes, then this book will give you an understanding of the steps you need to take to create a successful consulting business. I made the decision in 1994 and would never go back. GOOD LUCK!

Susan Nash

1

Defining Consulting

Business life is changing drastically and these changes are creating new opportunities in the business world. This book has been designed to provide a step-by-step introduction to qualified individuals who are considering entering the consulting profession. It will also help those who are uncertain about wanting to enter the consulting industry to decide whether it would suit them.

This first chapter will provide a brief introduction to organisations and the new world of work, and then describe how consulting fits into this business model.

THE BUSINESS ENVIRONMENT IN THE YEAR 2000 AND BEYOND

The business environment is moving from stability in earlier decades to radical, complex and increasing change. Thirty years ago companies saw the future as somewhat predictable and manageable with gradual incremental change. Change occurred in a linear fashion where one cause produced only one effect, with a simple additive property, e.g. $1 + 1 = 2$. Change now is being driven from a variety of perspectives and is happening exponentially. There are non-linear relationships among causes and effects, where there can be multiple solutions to one problem, and there is synergy with the interaction of the parts, e.g. $1 + 1 = 4!!$

Some of the causes of change in the business market are:

- global competition
- technological advances
- decreasing product life cycles
- multiple communication channels
- expectation of instant, 24-hour availability
- change from manual to cerebral skills (by the year 2000, 70 per

cent of all jobs in Europe and 80 per cent of all jobs in the USA will require cerebral skills)

- virtual elimination of 'jobs for life'.

In the past 20 years alone, the following changes have been recorded:

- In 1984 the average product development cycle was three years. In 1990 it was 18 months. In 1997 it was six months and dropping.

- In Singapore, during his or her lifetime, a graduate can expect to change careers three times and change jobs every four years.

- In 1996, the annual rate of growth for the World Wide Web was 314,000 per cent.

- According to the National Research Council, in 1996 it took 7–14 years for a worker's skills to become obsolete. Today, it takes only 3–5 years for 50 per cent of our skills to become outdated.

THE SHAMROCK ORGANISATION

As these changes are taking place, the 1980s and 1990s have seen a drastic restructuring in the economic workplace. This phenomenon has been described as 'atomising' where more and more smaller businesses are performing the work that fewer and larger organisations did before. Organisations have had to change the ways in which they operate in order to survive.

Charles Handy, in his book *The Age of Unreason*, talked about the Shamrock Organisation of the future which comprises three key components (see Figure 1):

- full-time knowledge workers with specialised expertise

- part-time, hourly or temporary workers who are flexible and provide less complex skills

- contract workers who also possess specialised expertise but who provide this on a consulting or contract basis.

This strategy provides organisations with greater flexibility, reduction in costs (ensuring full-time people are not employed in quiet times) and greater adaptability. This atomising has brought many changes

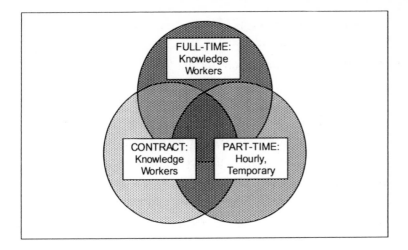

Fig. 1. The Shamrock Organisation.

to the way people work. Individuals have the choice of working full-time for an organisation or providing their services in a consulting arrangement.

The role of consulting is part of the third leaf of the shamrock. Consulting remains a lucrative growth industry for those who are able to innovate for their clients' benefit and it continues to be a productive outlet for thousands of solo practitioners who choose this profession over a 9-to-5 job working for someone else.

WHAT IS CONSULTING?

Consulting can be defined as **providing independent services to meet a variety of clients' needs in exchange for money**. The critical factor is money. There will always be lots of opportunities for helping clients, but ensuring these clients are willing to pay is critical. While some individuals believe that giving away services is a way to establish a client base and get started, you are devaluing your services by not charging for them. Free consulting generates lots of demand for...more free consulting!! Deciding to charge a lower rate to clients in the beginning stage of your business is a strategy we will discuss and evaluate in Chapter 7: Financing Your Business.

THE CONSULTING INDUSTRY

The consulting industry is diverse, unregulated and broken into several categories:

- Large national and multinational firms employing more than 50 consultants, e.g. strategic consulting firms such as McKinsey and Company and Bain and Company, the large accounting firms such as Arthur Andersen, Ernst and Young, etc.

- Medium-size firms employing between ten and 50 consultants.

- Individual practitioners. *Venture* magazine estimates that more than half of all consulting firms are one-person operations.

- Internal consultants. These consultants work with only one company's divisions, subsidiaries and new acquisitions. The money they receive is their salary.

- Individuals between jobs.

Types of consulting

The types of services that consultants provide will vary from industry to industry and individual to individual. Areas of expertise can include problem-solving, assessing needs, making recommendations, providing additional resources, and implementing ideas.

Consulting can be viewed as a state of mind: a common approach to a situation whether you are internal or external to an organisation. There are many different types of consultants. The following are definitions of but a few:

- strategic planning consultants who help organisations define their vision and direction

- process re-engineering consultants who provide support by evaluating and recommending process improvements

- training consultants who provide services such as training programmes and curriculum development

- computer consultants who may assess the efficiency of current systems, and recommend or implement improvements

- marketing consultants who help design new product improvements and design product launch strategies.

In fact, the following statement is often heard, 'If you can't do the work, teach. If you can't teach, consult!'

Consulting *v.* contracting

Consulting is defined as different from contracting because, among other things, consultants:

- help more than one client

- control their own output

- are not told how, just what

- have their own place of work

- are responsible for their own output

- market their services.

Consulting is growing as organisations focus on their areas of speciality and use consultants to provide additional services. According to Charles Handy, over 50 per cent of the population will be in the category of independent worker by the year 2000: temporary, consulting, self-employed, part-time, etc. Many consulting companies originate when organisations lay off individuals and then use their services on a contract basis. Oracle has its own consulting division, and yet many consulting companies have sprung up to supplement its services. Because of the many changes in the business industry, there are far more consultants today than ever before.

ADVANTAGES AND DISADVANTAGES OF WORKING FOR A CONSULTING FIRM

If you are not familiar with the consulting industry, working for a consulting firm can be a good way to get started. The advantages and disadvantages of doing so are listed below:

Advantages

- Marketing is done for you.

- Clients are given to you.

- Billing and collection of payment is done for you.

- There is regular, dependable money.

- You have an opportunity to learn the business.

- Other resources are available to you such as copying, stationery, office space and equipment, etc.

- You do not have to worry about taxes, as most consulting firms will pay you and deduct taxes at source.

Disadvantages
Many of the perceived disadvantages of ordinary full-time work are present, for example:

- There will be the same amount of politics as in any other organisation.

- It is just another job.

- The pay will not be as high.

- You will have no opportunity to select clients.

For the purposes of this book, we will be looking at consulting through the lens of establishing your own consulting business.

OBJECTIVES OF THIS BOOK

This book has been written for professionals, with specific functional knowledge, experience or expertise, who wish to evaluate whether they want to be consultants and to consider an alternative lifestyle to full-time work. It is not designed for individuals who are starting their career, or who are already working in consulting firms. After you have finished reading this book you will:

- have a clear understanding of consulting and your fit in the consulting business

- understand how to raise finances and maintain financial control of your business

- be able to create and implement your marketing strategy

- know how to establish a client base

- understand how to balance conducting on-going business and maintaining the marketing process

- know how to organise your consulting business.

APPROACH

Through the rest of the book we will introduce the principal concepts, knowledge and information you require, within specific areas, to become a successful consultant. Then we will use checklists and action points to help you implement the key ideas. In addition, we will follow three people as they evaluate whether they wish to be consultants, and as they make a start in the consulting profession.

Marie

Marie has been in the training business for over 15 years. She spent seven years with a training company, which grew from three people to 100, during which time she was in the sales and marketing function. When she left the training company, she worked for another company on the implementation side, running training programmes and designing curricula. She then joined a retail company as Director of Training but is wondering whether running her own training consulting firm would be a more lucrative and rewarding option.

Frank

Frank is a hardware engineer who has been working for a high-tech company for several years. As the technical support business became more challenging, with shorter product life cycles and more push to generate revenue instead of ensuring customer satisfaction, he decided to begin to evaluate different working options. He has begun to run classes for the local college on how to re-engineer support centres. He now has what appears to be a demand for his services on a contract basis and he wants to decide whether to start his own consulting company or to pass on the work to other colleagues who are currently independent.

Linda

Linda has spent many years in the corporate environment acting as a financial controller. She has worked in almost every market segment including retail, technology and distribution. She enjoys her work but has been frustrated by the experiences of several lay-offs and by always being in the cost control mode rather than a financial management position. She likes a secure environment but wishes to apply her skills in a more proactive context.

2

Evaluating Your Fit

Often when professionals consider consulting as a profession, they see only the money that other consultants charge and focus on the advantages of consulting as an alternative to corporate employment. In reality, running your own consulting business has certain advantages and disadvantages. It is important to understand and consider both to ensure you capitalise on the strengths and reduce and/or avoid the weaknesses. Being honest with yourself and keeping your eyes open will increase your chances of building a successful consulting business.

ADVANTAGES AND DISADVANTAGES OF CONSULTING

Below are listed some of the advantages and disadvantages that need to be carefully thought through when considering consulting as a full-time career.

Advantages
- flexibility in hours and clothes
- creativity in projects
- diversity in work
- higher pay (when working)
- able to work own hours to match body clock
- focus on work you like to do
- no performance reviews
- can choose work associates and environment
- fewer politics
- see the results of the work you do
- get paid for the work you do, not your political savvy
- higher challenges

- less constrained by a job description
- greater impact
- can save money for retirement
- in control of your own destiny
- project-oriented with a beginning, a middle and an end
- greater opportunities
- chance for continuous learning
- more time off.

Disadvantages
- uncertain and variable income – feast or famine
- hard to find clients
- always looking for work – constant marketing
- must perform all tasks: marketing, finance, etc.
- no work, no pay
- taxes can be a problem – time consuming and detail-oriented
- hard to get accurate feedback
- very vulnerable to business cycles
- many bosses
- must be self-motivated
- no holiday pay
- must be healthy
- must handle rejection
- lonely
- have to self-train and pay for any training you do
- can be like starting a new job every day
- pay your own private health care insurance
- no support services
- hard to leave work behind
- need to constantly shift between projects and other tasks.

Individuals who have experienced redundancies, lay-offs, etc. often view consulting as a 'miracle cure'. Take a moment and list below what you perceive to be the advantages and disadvantages of consulting **for you**.

Advantages	Disadvantages
_____	_____
_____	_____
_____	_____
_____	_____

DOES CONSULTING SUIT YOU?

Consulting is a demanding profession and the requirements for success are therefore also demanding. A study by the Association of Management Consultants entitled 'Personal Qualifications of Management Consultants' found the following attributes essential for successful consultants:

- understanding of people
- integrity
- courage
- objectivity
- ambition
- problem-solving ability
- judgement
- ability to communicate
- psychological maturity
- good physical and mental health
- professional etiquette and courtesy
- stability of behaviour and action
- self-confidence
- intellectual competence
- creative imagination.

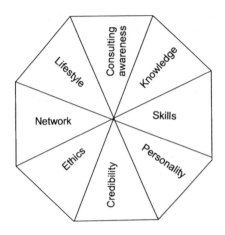

Fig. 2. Categories for successful consultants.

Robert E. Kelly, in his book *Consulting*, has summarised eight categories for successful consultants (see Figure 2).

1. Consulting process awareness
The first requirement is to understand that consulting is a process with a series of stages. Each stage has a series of tasks that must be performed (see Figure 3).

Fig. 3. Consulting process.

At any one time, you need to be marketing, meeting with prospects, writing proposals, 'doing the real work', billing, collecting revenue, keeping your office organised and ensuring your services are smoothly delivered. When you work for an organisation, you often only have to work in a couple of areas. Neglecting marketing when you are busy with a client can result in a shortfall in future income and the 'feast or famine' described by many consultants. Your understanding of, and your ability to work simultaneously in, all steps of the process are critical to your overall business success. Most consultants fail because they are unable to 'multiplex' adequately, and then neglect necessary aspects of their business.

2. Knowledge needed

In order to consult, you must have specific expertise, usually resulting from an in-depth knowledge of a particular industry, function or technique, for instance process re-engineering, training or finance. You also need broad business knowledge in such fields as accounting, market and competitor information, plus general knowledge of how organisations operate. Individuals who have worked for larger organisations often lack this broader business perspective.

3. Skills required

Most consultants have a specialised skill set. Successful consultants have all of the skills in the following major categories:

Technical/functional skills
You must have something of particular value to offer the client. This means an area of functional speciality such as marketing, product management, training, computer programming, human resources management, etc. These are the skills most individuals consider when considering consulting as a career option.

Communication/interpersonal skills
This is the ability to convey important information, in both oral and written form. Ninety per cent of a consultant's day is spent communicating. Without effective communication skills you will have no work. Specific communication skills include presentation skills, listening skills and negotiating and writing skills.

You also need interpersonal skills in order to manage effectively the behaviour of the client as well as yourself during the engagement. Many consultants fail because they can do the work but cannot communicate this ability to different clients.

Business management skills
This is the ability to understand the critical elements of running a business including administration, cash flow, marketing, etc.

Administrative/organisational skills
These are the skills necessary for managing projects and paperwork. With no organisation structure around you, you have to be able to institute your own administrative system, e.g. remembering to send an invoice is critical to earning money.

4. Personality
Consultants tend to be self-starters, with high energy levels, self-confidence and tolerance of ambiguity. They need to be curious and creative in order to help clients solve problems. Other important personality traits used to describe consultants are self-disciplined, empathetic, tenacious and detail-oriented. Consultants must also be independent and assertive and have a strong desire to persevere. With no set pattern of work, and no formal performance evaluation process, a consultant has to be strongly self-directed. A sense of humour is also a big help.

Individuals often use a detailed self-assessment process, such as the Myers Briggs Type Indicator (MBTI), to more fully understand and work with their innate preferences. As a consultant, you are what you sell, so self-knowledge is critical to running a successful business. You can also use self-knowledge to capitalise on your strengths and overcome your weaknesses.

Using Keirsey's book, *Please Understand Me*, will also enable you to more fully understand your innate needs and values. Each of us views the world through our own set of lenses and perceptions, distorting reality to match our own mental picture. We are all unique individuals with our own complexities and idiosyncrasies, but for 25 centuries, four basic patterns have been consistently and cross-culturally recognised in the human personality.

Temperament theory is based on four sets of themes. These sets serve as fractals of personality. A fractal is a pattern underlying seemingly random phenomena. Human personality is complex and varying, but temperament reveals the underlying inborn foundation on which personality is built. In temperament theory, we start with an understanding of the core themes and then examine our basic psychological needs, core values, favourite talents, common approaches and habitual worldview. People with the same temperament share the same core needs and values. This does not mean that these people are all the same. There are wide varieties, but with strong shared needs. For example, string instruments are a family of musical instruments, but there are huge differences between a guitar and a double bass!

Once we understand our own basic patterns, it becomes much easier to make more effective choices and communicate with those who are different. Let's look at these temperaments in more detail.

- **Artisans** live one day at a time, seizing the day and all the freedom they can get. They are the natural crisis managers and performers. They are opportunistic, act in the moment and need to make an impact on their environment. Functions to describe artisans' roles as consultants have included tacticians, trouble-shooters, fire-fighters and negotiators.

- **Guardians** are driven by responsibility and duty, wishing to serve and protect their loved ones. They are the pillars of society and need membership and belonging within a group. Types of work guardians fulfil as consultants are process improvement, statistical process control, re-engineering and quality management.

- **Rationals** seek knowledge and competence in all of their endeavours. They seek to understand the operating principles of everyone and everything around them. They need to create their own destiny. Types of services rational consultants provide include strategic planning, marketing, design and systems analysis.

- **Idealists** are soul-searchers who constantly quest for meaning and significance in their lives. They want to do something meaningful for this world and are constantly on a journey to find and be their unique self. Roles that idealists play as consultants include coaches, catalysts, advocates and facilitators.

5. Credibility

Clients want to use someone they can trust and therefore need proof of your trustworthiness. You can build credibility both by referring to your background and from your behaviour when you interact with the client. You can use accomplishments in previous jobs and referrals to establish trustworthiness when you are getting started. In addition, companies you have worked for in the past and job titles you have held can enhance your market standing. Your curriculum vitae (CV) can provide information on proven knowledge, skills or experience. In some consulting areas, specific qualifications can be used to prove expertise. For instance, if you are providing services in software, a PhD in computer science would enhance your credibility. You also build credibility by doing what you say you will do: if you say you will send information, do it. If you can't, call and explain why and try to negotiate a new deadline.

6. A code of ethics

Word travels fast. You are only as successful as your reputation. A code of ethics can help you guide your decisions as to what work to take or not take, and normally reflects such key values as the following:

- If you can't do the work, don't take the job.
- Respect the customer: the customer is always right, even when wrong.
- Perform regular examinations of the consulting practice.
- Have an open attitude towards a variety of people.
- Don't charge the customer for hours not worked.
- Deliver what you promise and a bit more.
- Don't criticise the competition.

For example, it can be tempting to take any assignment as you're starting out, but if you cannot deliver to a sufficient standard, it will be damaging to your credibility. The better solution in this case is to find someone else who can do the work: ultimately you get more work. In the consulting business, what goes around, comes around!

7. Networking

Consulting is a relationship sell. To survive as a consultant, you need to create personal and professional networks. These provide both a marketing base and a source of support, and are critical for building an on-going practice. You also need a network of fellow consultants to provide help with specific large projects or to fill in for you when necessary. As your network is such a key business development tool, more detail about networking is included in Chapter 5.

8. Lifestyles

A consultant's lifestyle may involve travel, long hours and pressure.

The benefits balancing this are a high degree of autonomy, the chance to help and influence others, and the possibility of high earnings, status and respect. Too many consultants are not prepared, nor do they have the support structure, for this lifestyle. It is important that your significant others understand the complexity of the process, realising that a day working at home is not a day off, and that working at home is still working. Building a support structure of other consultants in the business will give you someone to lean on when the occasional proposal is rejected. Don't kid yourself thinking you'll have lots of time off. You won't.

Put simply, as a consultant, you need to be able to:

- market your service

- deliver your service

- organise your administration

- be an accountant.

In order to assess whether consulting is for you, you must first thoroughly investigate the area in which you wish to consult and consider another few key pointers:

- Do something you really enjoy.

- Build a network; talk to as many people as you can in the business.

- Set realistic goals.

- Be patient.

Many consultants conduct a self-assessment in terms of their strengths and weaknesses in the eight critical categories, described above. Figure 4 is an example of a typical self-assessment. You can use the blank form in Figure 5 to rate yourself in the various categories.

Now that you have thought about your fit within the consulting industry, we will next look at how to get started planning your business. But first, take a few moments to review the checklist, case studies and action points.

Category	Your self-assessment
Consulting process awareness	Thorough knowledge of all steps from working for Bain and Company.
Knowledge	Functional knowledge in business process re-engineering. Good general business knowledge.
Skills	Excellent written communication skills. May have to work on interpersonal skills with clients – can tend to be too abrupt. Excellent organisation and follow-through skills.
Personality	Resourceful and independent minded. Persistent. Tend to get stressed when overloaded.
Credibility	Over ten years' consulting experience with major multinational organisations.
Ethics	Haven't thought about it – will need to consider prior to taking first assignment.
Network	Strong network for the organisation I worked for, but not for me. Have to investigate non-compete clauses.
Lifestyle	Not married so plenty of freedom. Know several other independent consultants for advice and insight if needed.

Fig. 4. Self-assessment – example.

Category	Your self-assessment
Consulting process awareness	
Knowledge	
Skills	
Personality	
Credibility	
Ethics	
Network	
Lifestyle	

Fig. 5. Self-assessment – form.

CHECKLIST

Is consulting for you?

1. Do you fully understand the consulting process?
2. Do you have functional skills or specialised content knowledge?
3. Do you have credibility as a consultant?
4. Does your personality fit?
5. Do you have a clearly defined code of ethics?
6. Do you have a good size network?
7. Does consulting fit your lifestyle?
8. Can you deliver the work?
9. Can you market the work?
10. Can you organise the work?
11. Can you budget to manage the ups and downs?
12. Is this work something you really enjoy?

CASE STUDIES

Marie has consulting experience

Marie has been in the training business both in a training-consulting firm and as Director of Training for a retail company, and is now considering starting her own consulting business. Her employment as Director of Training has definitely built her credibility. During her employment, she has also provided limited consulting services for other clients, negotiating time off without pay from her employer.

Because of her work with the training company, she has an excellent knowledge of the consulting process and possesses excellent sales and marketing skills. She has evaluated the advantages and disadvantages of consulting and believes that the benefits of reduced politics, greater challenge, control of the end product and variety of projects will overcome the potential disadvantages of needing a consistent revenue stream since both children are at university. She has a good family support structure that affirms her decision to 'go it alone'.

Having worked for a time management training company she feels confident in being able to organise her environment. As an idealist she is passionate about training and believes this can help motivate her in tough times.

Frank has excellent process re-engineering skills

Frank has worked for a major computer hardware and software manufacturer for over 20 years. During this time he has been able to attend lots of training programmes, work in many different departments and practise leading-edge process re-engineering. Though he has never done any consulting, he believes the advantages to him are more control over his own destiny, greater potential income and diversity of projects. He knows he has limited knowledge of the consulting process and marketing strategies, but he believes with his network of contacts and his experience he has enough basis to explore consulting as a career choice. He is a guardian and is excited by the opportunity to implement process improvements and see a project through from start to finish. He was recently divorced and has no financial responsibilities for children, so he thinks this is the best time to try out consulting.

Linda is an excellent accountant

Linda has spent 15 years in a variety of jobs in large organisations in different market segments from retail companies, to wholesale companies, to computer peripherals. She has played a variety of roles in the financial department including Manager of Accounts Payable, Manager of Accounts Receivable and Financial Controller. She believes her diverse experience can be more profitably used running her own consulting business. She has been through various reductions in force in three organisations as the companies have 'downsized', 'rightsized' and 're-engineered' her function, resulting in fewer people to do more work. She has seen some of her best friends and most capable colleagues forced into looking for new opportunities.

She believes she is now working so hard it would be easier to be a consultant than be an employee since she would at least have more flexible hours. She perceives that consultants who have helped her with projects are paid astronomical daily rates and she could do the work just as well. In addition, she wants to work in the training area, not just on financial projects. The benefits to her of consulting are:

- less exposure to corporate changes in direction
- greater flexibility
- fewer working hours.

As a rational, she believes her strategic expertise will be well received in most organisations. She realises she has very limited knowledge of the consulting process, is reluctant to market herself and does not have direct experience in the area in which she wishes to work (training). However, she has received the offer of a six-month severance package and wants to use that to get started.

ACTION POINTS

1. In terms of considering the advantages and disadvantages of consulting as a profession, have you created an objective list of pros and cons? Have you discussed this list with those who are close to you? Have you discussed the list with people who are consultants in your chosen area of practice?

2. In terms of the qualities of successful consultants, have you evaluated yourself against the categories? What are your critical competencies? Where do you rate yourself as lacking skills, knowledge or expertise? How can you capitalise on your competencies? How could you build capabilities where you perceive you may be exposed? How can you develop a support structure?

3

Getting Started and Building Key Result Areas

Often when individuals consider becoming consultants, they think of the logistical steps for getting started such as getting business cards, setting up the office, buying a computer, etc. But the first critical stage in starting your own practice is to define what you want your business to be. Most people begin with a vague notion of wanting to be a consultant, but it is very important to become specific. When people describe what they want to do, they make two main mistakes:

- First, they explain what they want to do in vague, long sentences.

- Second, they try to be a 'jack-of-all-trades' and not be tied to one area.

The first stage in starting your own practice is to be specific about your business direction by defining your **vision** for the future of your consulting business, identifying your **unique selling proposition**, and categorising the main responsibilities for your business (see Figure 6).

DEFINING YOUR VISION

What is a vision statement?

A vision can be defined as a picture of future greatness, a definition of core values, and a lighthouse towards the frontier. Your vision must make sense to others, stretch your imagination, give an 'aha' effect, but at the same time be within the bounds of possibility. Your vision statement describes the grand idea of what you are about and the future as you want it to be: 'I am in the business of...'. The vision statement must be reasonably precise yet still provide a general direction to your consulting business. The vision statement tends to be abstract, high level, and without much concrete detail. It has also been compared to the North Star: high above, constantly present, universally known, guiding direction. The purpose of your vision

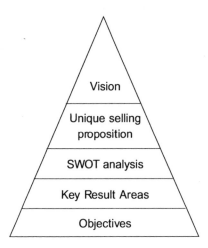

Fig. 6. Strategic planning pyramid.

statement is to guide your decision-making, provide a yardstick to keep you on track and provide inspiration in achieving your goals.

Examples of vision statements
Examples of vision statements from organisations are:

- **Oracle** – 'To enable the information age through network computing.'

- **Kepner Tregoe** – 'We focus on the human side of change though providing skills, development programmes and consulting services.'

- **Raychem** – 'To win the respect of our customers around the world by being a leader in delivering innovative solutions.'

Individuals' visions for their consulting businesses will be closely related to their temperaments. For example, vision statements for individual consulting firms could be:

- **Idealist** – 'To unleash the human potential in organisations.'

- **Rational** – 'To provide human resource expertise and solutions to enable organisations to meet their business objectives.'

- **Artisan** – 'To make an impact on sales and market share.'

- **Guardian** – 'To help organisations produce the best results.'

Other vision statements include:

- 'To unite Japan and the USA.'

- 'To help organisations optimise their marketing effectiveness.'

- 'To use creativity and innovations to help companies achieve their goals.'

Additional examples are also included in the case studies at the end of the chapter.

Differentiating between vision and mission statements
A mission statement communicates the vision by considering several critical variables:

- What is it the organisation wants to do?

- Who is the organisation's customer?

- What are our values?

- What profit do we need to make?

Raychem's mission statement for 1998 was to:

- sell $75 million in new products

- increase market share from 15 per cent to 17 per cent in heat tracing

- create new business opportunities.

When you are getting started in your consulting business, using only a vision statement, together with Key Result Areas, is probably adequate. Adding another level of detail may make the process too complex.

Creating your vision statement
Creating a vision statement will take you some time. Often the first ideas you come up with tend to be more detail-oriented. If this is the case you will need to continue refining the statement by talking to friends, professional acquaintances and prospective customers. Time

invested in this area will reap rewards for your business in the long term.

Other techniques to facilitate this process are to think of an ideal day: What would you do? Who would you work with? Where would you work? What would be the result?

Alternatively, think of some times when you felt really motivated: What were you doing? With whom? What made it motivational for you? It may be that you already have a personal vision statement that you can adapt to your business.

Common challenges that arise in trying to define a vision include being too specific, too 'pie in the sky', not able to share with customers, or appearing as if it is not related to the business.

Spend a few moments now and begin to define your vision.

_____

_____

_____

_____

_____

IDENTIFYING YOUR UNIQUE SELLING PROPOSITION

Your unique selling proposition is how you define your unique contribution within your chosen area of expertise. It identifies why someone should buy your services and not someone else's. It describes the value you can add to an organisation. It is a statement reflecting your competitive advantage.

Your unique selling proposition has both an internal and an external focus. For example, a trainer might claim his or her unique selling proposition (with an internal focus towards the business) is that he or she has excellent facilitation skills. The unique selling proposition from the customer's perspective (the external focus) is that the trainer has the ability to motivate small and large groups.

We are often unaware of our own strengths and competencies. Since they are natural to us we do not even think about them. In the grid in Figure 7, strengths fall into the quadrant entitled unconscious competence. In order to capitalise on our strengths we need to be aware of them.

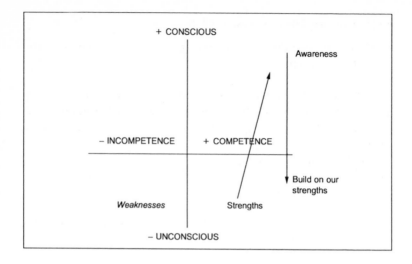

Fig. 7. Conscious/unconscious – competence/incompetence quadrant.

Strengths

Often our strengths are in unconscious competence. They are natural and we don't have to think about them to use them. If we are to be able to clearly articulate our unique selling proposition, we need to become aware of these strengths so we can capitalise and build on them.

The way you identify how your strengths manifest themselves in business is to review previous accomplishments and ask yourself what you did that was different from what others might have done, or what it was that you were able to uniquely contribute to the success of this project. For example, a Director of Training at a retail company rolled out a sales training programme to over 200 retail stores, resulting in a 16 per cent comparative store sales increase. The company had tried to roll out a sales training programme two years previously but it had not worked. When he asked himself the question 'What did I do that the previous Director of Training had not?' he identified the following factors that had uniquely contributed to the programme's success:

- He had obtained senior management commitment.

- He had involved the retail team in the development of the programme.

- He had simplified the design of the content.

- He had ensured there were follow-up strategies in place to ensure continuity of change.

From this he deduced that part of his unique selling proposition was his ability to accurately identify customer needs, tailor an appropriate solution to those needs and thereby ensure the solutions were commercially viable.

Asking friends, previous employers and professional peers for their insight can provide other useful data in documenting your unique selling proposition.

Spend a few moments now and identify the critical components of your unique selling proposition.

_____

_____

_____

_____

_____

Your vision and unique selling proposition are valuable, in terms both of the direction they provide to your business, and their use in marketing your business. While the process of defining them is difficult, it is a critical step in your journey towards creating your own successful consulting business. Make sure you revisit defining your vision and identifying your unique selling proposition until they are accurate.

SWOT ANALYSIS

SWOT analysis means taking a probing look at the Strengths, Weaknesses, Opportunities and Threats that face your consulting business. The analysis is a process of investigating and brainstorming the factors working for and against your practice that could affect overall performance. Strengths and weaknesses refer to your business's internal advantages and potential disadvantages. These factors are in your direct control. Opportunities and threats refer to aspects outside your direct control that might open up potential (opportunities) or result in negative consequences (threats). Opportunities and threats can originate either in the market at large or from your competitors.

The purpose of SWOT analysis is to view the world in which you are performing from a macro perspective. This vantage point ensures that the planned strategy and direction are possible, given your inherent strengths and weaknesses. It also ensures that the strategy is geared towards capitalising on opportunities and minimising threats.

Examples from a SWOT analysis undertaken by a training and development consultant were as follows:

Strengths
- 20 years' experience.
- Excellent network of contacts.
- Specialised functional expertise in Situational Leadership^{TM} and Break It Thinking^{TM} (training programmes).
- Great marketing skills.
- Package of programmes available to sell.
- Organised.

Weaknesses
- Lack of administrative support.
- Lack of procedures.
- Limited financial resources.
- Too many customised programmes.
- Inadequate resource of alternative trainers.

Opportunities
- Thriving market.
- Companies are downsizing making more demand for contract trainers.
- More companies are outsourcing trainers.
- Many business publications talk about the importance of developing human potential as critical to an organisation's success.

Threats
- Growth in alternative training delivery methodologies such as computer-based training may reduce the demand for 'classroom' training.
- There are many one-person consulting firms.
- Future financial market stability.

- Difficulty in raising market awareness.
- Changing company strategies and people moving from one company to another.

Spend a few moments now conducting a SWOT analysis for your consulting business.

Strengths

_____

_____

Weaknesses

_____

_____

Opportunities

_____

_____

Threats

_____

_____

UNDERSTANDING KEY RESULT AREAS

Deciding what is important

While many consultants set objectives for their business, often there is no direct link between the business's vision/unique selling proposition and the tasks that have to be completed on a day-to-day basis. In fact, often you have what appears to be a never-ending list of projects, while what you do day-to-day is not represented at all. As a result you appear as though you are not performing and become overloaded and stressed.

Establishing Key Result Areas is a valuable technique that links the overall direction of your consulting practice with project goals and current milestones. Key Result Areas reflect the most important areas of responsibility of the consulting business, the areas in which results must be achieved. This grouping procedure is a valuable tool in managing workload as the process complements the way the human brain naturally works.

Building an overview of the brain

Our brains are structured into three levels of consciousness:

Subconscious brain

The subconscious brain works 24 hours a day and has, as far as we know, unlimited capacity. The challenge with the subconscious brain is that it is a random access device – in other words, it has no filing system from which we can easily call up information.

Conscious brain

The conscious brain works only when we are awake and it can concentrate on only one thought at a time. As a result, when we have a multitude of tasks to complete we feel overloaded.

Preconscious brain

The third level of the brain, the preconscious, helps us out by keeping track of an effective overview. The preconscious brain can keep an outline of seven $+/-$ two, i.e. five to nine categories. If you can create a list of approximately seven areas of responsibility covering all aspects of your consulting business, you will be able to set realistic goals and milestones more effectively.

Being productive

Productivity means accomplishing goals and achieving results. If you are to achieve your overall goals, you need to clearly visualise them and spend your time on the right things, your Key Result Areas. Highly productive consultants carefully focus their planning and management of activities around Key Result Areas. They *choose* to make these a constant priority and manage other responsibilities *after* these key areas are taken care of.

Key Result Areas are the most important areas of your business and therefore results must be achieved within those areas. They are your main areas of responsibilities. They are where you need to concentrate your time to achieve your goals. They do *not* describe the type of results to be achieved nor how you will achieve them.

Key Result Areas are **headings** and therefore are described by **nouns**. They do not answer the what, when, how or how much questions, so avoid the use of verbs to describe them.

Defining Key Result Areas

- *Be brief.* Use a maximum of 1–4 words.

- *Use headings.* Key Result Areas should be headings that describe areas within which results are to be achieved. They should not state specific aims or performance standards.

- *Be complete.* Your Key Result Areas should cover *all* aspects of your business – all you do and ought to do needs to be included somewhere in a Key Result Area.

- *Be clear.* Key Result Areas should be immediately understandable.

- *Avoid overlapping.* Where two Key Result Areas are just different aspects of the same subject, they should be combined into one.

Examples of Key Result Areas for a Business Manager
- Finance
- Sales
- Marketing
- Team development
- Customer service
- Operations
- Communication
- Reporting
- Project management.

Other examples
- Projects
- Quality
- Research and development
- Manufacturing
- Vendor management
- Purchasing
- Process improvement
- Problem identification.

ESTABLISHING YOUR KEY RESULT AREAS

There are various approaches to identifying your Key Result Areas. Start by identifying the overall requirements of your business. Ask yourself the question, '**Which main areas (Key Result Areas) should I concentrate my efforts on to reach my goals?**'

The Key Result Areas represent the **critical few** areas where you target results. Limit them to no more than ten. This focus will make it easier for you to maintain overview and keep control.

In addition, you can ask yourself the following questions:

- Where do I need to pay attention in order to keep an edge on my business?

- What results am I expected to achieve?

- What activities bring recognition or challenges?

- How do I spend my time?

- In which areas can I work to create specific results for my company and/or myself?

- What will create the future for my consulting business?

Understanding your workload

Brainstorm a list of tasks covering your workload. Then categorise this list into no more than nine Key Result Areas. For example, you might have ideas like:

- Brainstorm list of contacts.

- Write a business plan.

- Do market research.

- Define product/service.

- Talk to people who said they would help me out.

- Do budget.

- Get computer and software.

- Buy furniture.

These tasks could be grouped under different headings:

Marketing
- Do market research.
- Define product/service.

Networking
- Brainstorm list of contacts.
- Talk to people who said they would help me out.

Administration/set up
- Get a computer and software.
- Buy furniture.

Financial control
- Write a business plan.
- Do a budget.

By grouping the tasks in this way you enable the brain to build an overview of tasks, thereby reducing stress and providing a better basis for prioritising activities.

Determining Key Result Areas

Figure 8 lists the Key Result Areas for most consulting businesses. Figure 9 has been left blank for you to fill in your own Key Result Areas.

Once you have defined the overall direction for your business, you need to be more specific in establishing your business plan. This will be the subject covered in Chapter 4. Spend a few minutes now reviewing the checklist, case studies and action points.

CHECKLIST

1. Have you created an initial vision statement?

2. Have you identified your unique selling proposition?

3. Have you listed three people who could give you advice on your vision and unique selling proposition?

4. Have you conducted an initial SWOT analysis for your business?

5. Have you defined the Key Result Areas for your business?

CASE STUDIES

Marie gets started

Marie defined her vision as 'To provide training and consulting services to allow individuals and teams to maximise results'. Although the statement is a little long, she believes the vision encompasses the critical direction of her business: the key words are training, consulting, individuals, teams and results. She would have preferred to say 'develop their potential' but she thinks that these

MY KEY RESULT AREAS
1 Financial Control
2 Clients   A.   B.   C.
3 Business Development
4 Database Management/Marketing
5 Product Development
6 Organisational Effectiveness/Administration
7 Team Development
8 Professional Development

Fig. 8. Key Result Areas – example.

MY KEY RESULT AREAS
1
2
3
4
5
6
7
8
9

Fig. 9. Key Result Areas – form.

words might not be acceptable in the business community.

She has categorised her unique selling proposition as 'Being a business person first and a trainer second which means that all services are practical and bottom-line oriented.'

When she conducted the SWOT analysis for her business, she realised that although a strength of her business was breadth of services, this might also produce an associated weakness from not adequately focusing the business and trying to be all things to all people. As a result of this analysis, she has decided to focus on team development as her primary business interest. She knows that she will probably have to do other projects in the early stages of her business, but plans that this will be her ultimate direction.

Her Key Result Areas are:

- Client/project management
- Prospects
- Marketing activities
- Product development
- Administration
- Financial control
- Networking
- Professional development.

Frank gets started

Frank defined his vision as 'To help call centres optimise their productivity'. He believes this provides a good overall direction, but does not limit him to only process re-engineering. Key words in his vision statement are call centres (this could include technical support and customer service centres), optimise and productivity. He wants to ensure that any work he conducts will have a tangible bottom-line effect on the company. 'If it does not make a difference at 9:00 a.m. on a Monday morning, I will not have succeeded.' He believes that working for large organisations is where he can add the most value.

He believes his unique selling proposition is, 'A technically competent engineer who can accurately improve call centre operations'. He believes many engineers, while they possess the technical skills to undertake process re-engineering, lack the interpersonal skills required to build relationships and communicate the key changes required.

In his SWOT analysis, he identified as opportunities the huge growth in call centres, but highlighted as a possible weakness/threat the challenges of being a small player in such a huge, unregulated market. He realises he will have to use creative marketing channels to be able to successfully launch his business.

His Key Result Areas are very similar to Marie's:

- Target companies
- Business development
- Marketing activities
- Product development
- Logistics
- Financial control
- Networking
- Professional development.

Linda gets started

Linda struggled with writing her vision statement. Every time she tried to articulate her vision as a statement that covered not only her existing areas of expertise, but also the new area she wished to research, the end result always sounded too task-focused. To this point she has defined her vision as 'To provide consulting services to help organisations optimise their financial resources'.

In addition, because she wants to diversify into an area where she has no direct experience, she is having problems identifying her unique selling proposition. She also does not fully comprehend the term. She thinks that there are no true black and white differences among consultants and to say so is inaccurate. Her initial idea for her unique selling proposition is, 'Experienced, well-rounded accountant, with the ability to improve the use of financial resources through better use of both people and systems'.

She defined her Key Result Areas as:

- Office set-up
- Networking
- Market research
- Financial budget
- Business plan.

Her Key Result Areas tended to appear task-focused instead of category-focused.

ACTION POINTS

1. As you define your vision and unique selling proposition, whom else can you talk to for feedback? What other resources could you use to give you examples and ideas? By what date do you wish to finalise your vision and unique selling proposition?

2. As a result of your SWOT analysis, what specific threats or weaknesses did you find that might inhibit the future performance of your consulting business? What specific strengths and opportunities did you identify that would help you to build your consulting business? What plans have you put in place to ensure you follow through with your initial ideas?

3. As you define your Key Result Areas, are they representative of your entire workload? Do the headings make sense and provide you with an accurate overview of your workload? Are they in alignment with your vision and unique selling proposition?

4

Establishing Your Business Direction

Once you have established your vision and unique selling proposition, conducted your SWOT analysis and defined the Key Result Areas for your consulting business, it is critical to write in more detail what you specifically wish to accomplish and how you will do this. For this purpose, we normally create a business plan, organise ourselves legally and then define specific objectives and milestones.

WRITING A BUSINESS PLAN

The business plan performs three major functions:

1. It forces you to think through each aspect of your business while keeping you focused and structured. It also helps set limits.

2. It allows a dry run before you actually perform your first consulting assignment, e.g. it exposes you to potential sales, profits and problems.

3. It becomes a sales tool for both you and your potential investors.

Business plans vary in length and nature and basically comprise several main sections. For in-depth discussions of business plans, *New Venture Creation* and *Up Your Own Organization* provide excellent details (see Further Reading). Generally, a business plan should be from two to four pages. It should be a good guide, but not so complex that you don't want to change it, because it *will* change.

The sections of a typical business plan are based around the planning stages you have used for your business and will therefore include the following:

- **Cover page**. Name of company, address, phone and date.

- **Introductory summary**. This is a summary of the important information included in your business plan. Write the summary after you have written the entire plan. If you ask investors for money, they will want to read your business plan. They often read the introductory summary and decide, based on this section alone, whether to read the rest.

- **Table of contents**. This lets the reader know what is included in your business plan.

- **Your company overview.**

- **Vision statement, as you defined in Chapter 3.**

- **Unique selling proposition, as you defined in Chapter 3.**

- **SWOT analysis**. A seasoned businessperson realises that every venture entails risks. What are the possibilities of competitive responses to your actions? Are there unfavourable trends in the industry? Use a SWOT analysis to help you calculate your risks:
  - strengths for your business (internal)
  - weaknesses for your business (internal)
  - opportunities in the marketplace (external)
  - threats in the marketplace (external).
  SWOT analysis is discussed in detail in Chapter 3.

- **Key Result Area: financial control**.
  - *Financial plan*. Your financial plan identifies the sources and uses of your money in your business. It shows your financial standing through two basic documents, the profit and loss forecasts and the cash flow statements. This approach is covered in more detail in Chapter 7.
  - *Financial funding*. After determining how much money you need through your profit and loss and cash flow, your business plan needs to indicate where the money will come from.

- **Key Result Area: marketing**.
  - *Market research*. This is a crucial section in the business plan. Many consultants enamoured of their own good idea fail to investigate whether there is a market for it.
  - *Market analysis*. In your market analysis you identify your expected major clients, estimate your potential annual sales to each and assess your potential market share. While this market assessment may be to a large extent theoretical in the early stages, it nonetheless serves to focus and direct your energies.
  - *Marketing plan*. The marketing plan gives a picture of the

market, your marketing goals, promotional strategies, who the competition is, what you will charge for your services and your strategy for finding customers.

- **Key Result Area: team development.**
  - *Management team.* The management team is responsible for making your business successful. If you are a sole practitioner, then you are the management team and perform all the major tasks for planning, marketing, accounting, financing, organising and consulting. Some consultants establish an adviser(s) to act as a sounding board for strategies and business opportunities. Your adviser can be someone from your previous job, an associate you respect or a businessperson you pay for his or her expertise. The arrangement can be as formal or informal as you want to make it.
  - *Professional assistance.* You should quickly establish relationships with necessary professionals such as a solicitor, an accountant, a banker and an insurance agent. Capable professionals provide significant part-time assistance when you are a sole practitioner.
  - *Other resources.* You should develop a team of other consultants, e.g. technical writers, editors, trainers, etc. to have on hand when you need help with projects. You may also get work from them when they need help.

- **Key Result Area: professional development.**
  - *Research and development.* Research and development appears in many forms and has costs associated with it. It can include such things as researching training materials, researching process improvements, writing books or developing new services to meet clients' needs.

- **Key Result Area: business development.**
  - *Target clients.* To reach your estimated sales projections you must develop a strategy that targets specific clients with specific sales approaches and determines which aspects of your firm's services you will stress in your marketing efforts.

- **Key Result Area: administration.**
  - *Logistics.* Listing of office set-up, processes, etc.

- **Key Result Area: product development.**
  - *Defining your product/service.* Being successful requires a clear understanding of your services and the potential benefits they

can provide to the customer. More information is included in a later chapter.

- **Overall schedule**. Your schedule pinpoints the timing and interrelationships of all the major events important to starting and developing your business. Some people use flow charts to visualise the process of starting, operating and planning for a growing business. It should also include your tasks and milestones.

Making time to complete the business plan will ensure that you are taking the right steps to build your consulting business and will not get side-tracked in other areas.

DECIDING YOUR LEGAL STRUCTURE

The most common legal structures for a consulting business are the sole proprietorship/trader, the partnership and the limited company. The structure you choose will be related to your overall business objectives. Make sure you talk to a solicitor to gather more specific information about your chosen field.

Sole proprietorships/traders

Most consulting businesses are sole proprietorships. Under this arrangement, you and your business are one and the same. If you use your name as the business name, you do not have to file under the assumed business name status. Your firm's net income is taxable as your personal income. You have an unlimited liability for the debts of your firm.

This type of business organisation is simple, yet effective as you are starting your consulting business. Even if you want to work with another person, it is often better to begin the co-operation as two sole traders. This gives you an opportunity to 'try out' the working relationship, before formalising a partnership. Unfortunately, there are a lot more broken partnerships than successful ones!

Partnerships

There are two types of partners, general and limited. General partnership partners control the day-to-day operations of the firm and usually have unlimited liability for the firm's debts. Limited partners, also known as silent partners, exercise no control over daily operations. They typically invest money in return for a share of the firm's profits.

Many individuals, who have worked together very successfully in a corporation, fail when they try to work together as partners. There are a variety of reasons for this:

- When working in an organisation, the payment does not depend on the working relationship. Often partners split up because there is not enough business for both partners: one can generate business, but can't do the work. The other can do the work but cannot generate business. This creates ill feelings between them.

- Working in a formal organisation structure, there are defined standards and procedures. Working in a partnership, individuals have to define their own structure and they may approach this process differently.

- If the partners are not clear when defining roles and responsibilities, it can result in frustration and disappointment between partners because one feels the other is not doing his or her job.

- Working together, 'on top of each other', is different from working in an organisation where there are other individuals present also.

So think carefully before you make this large commitment. Lawyers tend to make more money from partnerships than individuals do!

Limited companies

These are generally legal entities separate and distinct from you as an individual. Most larger businesses are limited companies. This brings several advantages including permanence, continuing despite the death of individual shareholders, and your personal liability is limited to the amount invested in stock. However, corporations have several disadvantages in that they are typically subject to higher taxes and fees, and the procedures, reports and statements required by the government may become cumbersome. See below for more information on the tax advantages and disadvantages of a limited company.

TAX AND OTHER FINANCIAL IMPLICATIONS

It is important to consult with your accountant regarding tax allowances, etc. The tax advantages and disadvantages and other financial implications of the different business structures are summarised below:

Sole trader

Advantages
- You can claim direct expenses related to the business such as telephone, heat, light, car, meals, etc. Check with your financial adviser for specific deductions allowed currently.

- You can use personal pension schemes to reduce tax liability.

- Often, if you work from home, you reduce travel time and expenses. When you do travel for the client you get these costs reimbursed.

- This is the simplest structure when working independently.

Disadvantages
- You are responsible for tracking costs and revenue, and filing tax returns bi-annually.

- You pay National Insurance contributions but you are not eligible to claim unemployment benefits.

- If you are sick, or have an illness in the family, your business may be exposed and you may have inadequate financial resources.

Partnership

Advantage
- You have someone else who shares tax liability.

Disadvantage
- Apart from the complexity of deciding separate tax bills, there are no additional disadvantages.

Limited company

Advantages
- There is a limit to corporation tax on profits up to £200,000.

- Company pension schemes for 'owner directors' are more generous in terms of tax relief than for an individual.

- Advantage can be made of additional business deductions such as company cars, although these are less beneficial now than previously.

Disadvantage
- There are more stringent reporting requirements than for a sole trader.

DEFINING OVERALL GOALS

A goal is a general statement of direction. A goal often does not have measurements and specific details. Generally you will have one overall goal for your consulting business. Specific outcomes/deliverables that contribute to this goal are defined using objectives.

SETTING OBJECTIVES

Once you have established your Key Result Areas, written your business plan and decided your legal structure, it is critical to write objectives for your business, and create a list of milestones to ensure you make progress to reach them.

What is an objective?
Objectives are concrete, tangible, measurable results or outcomes from your efforts that you can see, not just roles or activities. Well-clarified objectives, according to Alan Lakein, need to meet certain specific **SMART** criteria:

S – Specific, so that you know when you have achieved it.
M – Measurable by two or more of the following:
  – quality specifications (efficient? effective? other?)
  – cost.
A – Aligned with your overall vision and business direction.
R – Results-focused. Is a tangible result expected of me to produce/accomplish?
T – Time-based, with a specific due date.

Too often, we confuse tasks with objectives. A **task** is the action we must take, in order to reach the objective. To differentiate between tasks and objectives, you must ask yourself:

- What are you trying to achieve by completing this task?
- What is the benefit of achieving this task?

Make sure you use words such as ensure, increase, reduce, obtain, achieve, attain, raise, etc. in your objective statements.

Example
Incorrect
To contact five prospects by 31 January, 200X.

This is a task, and it does not tell us what the result is, or why we are doing this.

Correct
To obtain one client by contacting five prospects for training services, with revenue of £xxxxx by 31 January, 200X.

You can see that this is an effective objective because it is:

- Specific: one client
- Measurable: size of revenue
- Aligned: with the vision
- Results-focused: the result not the task
- Time-based: by 31 January, 200X.

Sometimes it is hard to be specific when writing subjective objectives. For example, when considering raising market awareness, it's hard to quantify this in a diverse, non-documented market such as process reengineering. In this case, tasks can be used as the measurement device, e.g. number of newsletters, advertisements, etc.

It is critical to define and write down objectives for every aspect of your business, within each Key Result Area. Research conducted on Harvard students 20 years after they had graduated showed that 5 per cent were earning more money than the other 95 per cent combined. The only difference was that the 5 per cent had **written down their objectives** after graduation. There is something about writing down objectives that affirms our commitment to them, and keeps them in sight and in mind.

The characteristic that gets missed the most when writing objectives is the **T** (time-based). Most people state vague terms such as 'within three months'. This is not specific enough – an actual date needs to be set. If the worst happens, and you do not succeed within the time frame, you can simply move the date!

Figure 10 gives examples of one objective for each Key Result Area for a consulting business. Remember there may be multiple objectives within each Key Result Area, and we will be showing more detail for each Key Result Area in later chapters.

As you will see, some Key Result Areas are easier to measure (finance) than others (database). In these situations the tasks and milestones have provided measurement criteria.

KEY RESULT AREAS AND OBJECTIVES	
Overall Goal:	To operate a thriving consulting business.
Key Result Area	**Objective(s)**
Finance	To achieve £200,000 in sales with a gross margin of 50% by 31 December, 200X.
Clients	To maintain an active client list of five current clients in 200X with no more than 50% income from one client. Client is defined as over £10,000 invoiced per year. An active client uses services at least once a quarter.
Business Development	To ensure five new clients in 200X with a pipeline of 10 prospects and 20 suspects as categorised on the database. Current clients are Oracle, etc.
Database Management	To establish and maintain a database of 200 contacts on ACT^{TM}, all personally known, by 31 December, 200X. To categorise the database by general, suspect and prospect. To maintain contact with the database by distributing three, eight-page newsletters and holiday greeting cards.
Product Development	To develop and roll out to three clients a 'Making Communication Work' seminar by 1 August, 200X.
Operational Effectiveness	To maximise operational effectiveness by updating filing system, and implementing new equipment (scanner) by 30 June, 200X.
Team Development	To establish an ongoing team by December 200X. Team comprises: • 2 Course Developers • Accountant • Office Manager • Finance Manager
Professional Development	To become certified in MBTI, by attending three workshops in 200X.

Fig. 10. Key Result Areas and objectives – example.
Are the objectives SMART: Specific, Measurable, Aligned,
Results-focused, Time-based?

KEY RESULT AREAS AND OBJECTIVES	
Overall Goal:	
Key Result Area	**Objective(s)**
1	
2	
3	
4	
5	
6	
7	
8	
9	

Fig. 11. Key Result Areas and objectives – form.
Are your objectives SMART: Specific, Measurable,
Aligned, Results-focused, Time-based?

Within each major objective there will be short-term 'sub-objectives', normally set on a quarterly basis. Short-term objectives are usually less than three months in duration, and can often be part of another larger objective. For instance, the client objective is part of the overall client management Key Result Area, and there will be multiple objectives for clients as the business grows.

Figure 11 has been left blank for you to fill in the Key Result Areas you identified in Chapter 3. For each, fill in one objective to measure your success in each area.

ESTABLISHING MILESTONES

When you have established and prioritised your objectives, it is important to decide the key tasks (the things you need to do) and milestones (delivery/completion dates) required to achieve the objectives. Where your objectives represent your destination, milestones represent the critical road map required to reach that destination. Without these tasks and milestones, there is a gap between what you want to do (the objective), and when you are going to do it (the plan). Failure to establish milestones is usually the key reason why we fail to achieve our objectives. We have to create a list of milestones **for every objective that we have** (see example in Figure 12).

For one of your current Key Result Areas, spend some time defining the objective(s) and considering what the critical tasks and milestones are. Use Figure 13 to record your conclusions.

Consultants vary on the **tools** they use to track their milestones and activities. Some use a paper-based system such as Filofax^{TM}. Others use software programs such as Microsoft Project^{TM}. Others will create a whiteboard and list all the projects and milestones on it so that they are in sight and in mind. (It's just a little heavy to carry to meetings!)

The system you use is not important: the thought process and the organisation of the data is key. If the milestones are not written down, first they are easier to forget, and second, you underestimate how many tasks there are at any one time. Finally, you also reduce stress on your brain by having them listed and not struggling to try to remember them.

You've now written your business plan, decided what legal structure to use, and established your Key Result Areas, objectives and

Key Result Area	Objective			
Database Management	To establish and maintain a database of 200 contacts on ACT™, all personally known, by 31 December, 200X.			
	To categorise the database by general, suspect and prospect.			
	To main contact with the database by distributing three, eight-page newsletters, and holiday greeting cards.			

Tasks and milestones necessary to complete the objective:

Number	What	Who	When	Completed
1	Brainstorm a list of contacts: • friends • family • employers • vendors.	SN	4/30/0X	
2	Research database sales tracking system.	DN	5/14/0X	
3	Select sales tracking system.	DN	5/31/0X	
4	Install sales tracking system.	DN	6/14/0X	
5	Input all names on new software.	DN	6/14/0X	
6	Categorise database into general, suspect and prospect.	SN	6/21/0X	

Fig. 12. Establishing milestones – example.

milestones, so we will move on to marketing your business which is the topic covered in Chapter 5. But first spend a few minutes reviewing the checklist, case studies and action points.

CHECKLIST

1. Have you created your business plan?

2. Have you reviewed the different legal structures and decided which one you will use?

3. Have you consulted with a tax adviser to ensure you understand the implications of this structure?

4. Have you defined objectives for at least three of your Key Result Areas?

Key Result Area	Objective(s)			
Tasks and activities necessary to complete the objective:				
Number	**What**	**Who**	**When**	**Completed**
1				
2				
3				
4				
5				
6				

Fig. 13. Establishing milestones – form.

5. Have you defined milestones for at least three of these objectives?

6. Have you chosen which system you will use to organise your projects and milestones?

CASE STUDIES

Marie gets organised

Marie has decided to get started as quickly as possible and has decided to organise herself as a sole trader. She believes this will give her flexibility in the short term, and she can decide at a later date if she wishes to incorporate. She has written a simple business plan following the outline in the materials for her own use only, as she does not want to use external funding to start the business. She has defined some key short-term objectives for herself. These include:

- Obtaining one client, for team training, paying no less than £5,000, within three months of today's date, by contacting 20 key prospects.

- Deciding an appropriate fee rate by researching five other independent training consultants, in order to establish market rates by 1 January, 200X.

- Ensuring a productive office by purchasing a new computer by 31 December, 200X, with ACT^{TM}, and the Microsoft Office Suite^{TM}.

She uses her Time Manager^{TM} system to list her objectives and milestones. Because she is familiar with the system, she believes this is the best way to keep the overview of her business. She has defined her critical milestones and is ready to start marketing her business.

Frank creates his business plan

Frank is more deliberate in his approach than Marie. He has also decided to do business as a sole trader, because he is not sure if he will remain as a consultant or not, and wishes to keep his options open. He has begun the process of creating a structured business plan, but he wishes to invest more time in this area to ensure that he is clear on his overall direction. His top two short-term objectives are:

- Ensuring a cohesive strategy by finalising a business plan by 31 December, 200X, that will be eight pages in length, including a finalised vision and unique selling proposition, SWOT analysis and Key Result Areas with critical objectives and tactics outlined.

- Establishing a prospective database of 200 contacts recorded on ACT^{TM} and categorised according to priority.

Frank has created a project plan on Microsoft Project^{TM} showing Key Result Areas, objectives and milestones, so he can identify and track inter-dependencies to ensure smooth progress for achieving his goals.

Linda sets her business direction

Linda also wishes to spend an extended period of time on her business plan. She likes to have a plan in place before she takes action and so does not want to rush in front of clients before she is ready. She finds it difficult to project her plan accurately into the future without knowing what work she will be doing, so she has bought two books and a software package to design a business plan. She has worked with another person in the past who is already a consultant, and she is considering joining her and creating a partnership. Linda has identified her two short-term goals as follows:

- Make a decision about partnership by 31 December, 200X, by researching legal issues and talking to other consultants who are partners.

- Finalise the business plan by 31 January, 200X.

Linda has enjoyed using the Palm Pilot™ to keep her organised. She has put all her phone numbers in the database and is entering the critical action items to track. The challenge with this tool is that it is not very good at providing an overview of the workload. So she is struggling to track progress in all areas (marketing and sales) as well as logistical and business actions.

ACTION POINTS

1. What software or books do you intend to purchase to help you write your business plan? How long do you believe your plan needs to be in order to provide you with enough direction, and yet not be too complex? Who else could provide advice in drawing up this plan? Will you use the plan as a tool to help you raise capital?

2. In terms of your organisation structure, what structure will be the most suitable for your needs in the short term? What other resources do you need to support you in this endeavour? How will you ensure you are organised well enough to avoid tax penalties?

3. When you review your objectives, how clear are they as to the result that they will achieve? Who could look at them and provide you with feedback to ensure they meet the SMART criteria? Are there clear benefits from the objectives?

4. What system will you use to track your milestones and tasks? When will you set up this system? How will you ensure that you keep this system current?

5

Marketing Your Business

Marketing your services is the next critical step in establishing a successful consulting business and will represent one of your Key Result Areas. Within this Key Result Area will be not only objectives related to deciding an overall marketing plan, but also how to use promotional strategies to raise awareness and build interest, and targets for creating a network from which to develop future opportunities.

CREATING YOUR MARKETING PLAN

Purpose of the plan

The marketing plan is a high-level statement, which reflects the overall direction of your business and includes information on the four Ps: Product, Price, Place and Promotion. We will discuss pricing strategies in detail in Chapter 7.

The purpose of your marketing plan is to provide your consulting business with an organised step-by-step approach for raising market awareness.

The key elements of your marketing plan are as follows:

- conducting market research
- establishing marketing objectives
- segmenting the market
- defining your product or service
- deciding your promotional plan
- creating a schedule.

Conducting market research

It is essential to conduct market research, not only into the type of consulting you wish to do, but also into the other companies that exist in that marketplace. Market research can be conducted before you leave your current position, and provides an ideal way of 'testing the water'. However, the extent to which quantitative market research is possible depends on the focus of your consulting business. Much of the consulting market comprises individual consultants and therefore it is hard to quantify and document it in detail. Objectives for market research are as follows:

- To identify whether there is a market for your product or service, and the possible size of your target market.

- To assess the existence, size and location of other competitors in your market.

- To discover the current pricing structure in your market.

- To identify corporate needs.

- To evaluate the best way to package your product or service for the market.

- To be used as a beginning for the business development process. Many consultants find their first client this way.

Depending on the focus of your business, both formal and informal approaches can be used in the market research process. Formal processes are designed to measure the size and potential market penetration of your service. Informal approaches are designed to obtain a subjective assessment of market potential. **Techniques** you can use are:

- Hire a consultant who specialises in market research to conduct the research for you. You can pay him or her, or organise some type of barter system in exchange for his or her services.

- Buy a mailing list for your potential market and distribute a questionnaire to the names on the list about your product or service. Remember the average return rate on such a survey is very small – less than 2 per cent. The questionnaire can be followed up by a phone call, which will increase the response rate and the success of the market assessment.

- Create a mailing list of people you know in the industry and send them a questionnaire. You can either ask that the questionnaire be returned, or ask to meet directly with them to obtain their feedback.

- Call contacts whose opinions you respect, and conduct a short phone interview with them. In this telephone interview, you could ask such questions as: 'If you were in my shoes, what would you do?', 'Who do you think would be interested in the services?', 'What else might they be interested in?'

- Research trade associations in your field and either attend meetings for networking reasons or use their list of members to target for research.

- Attend cocktail parties and other social functions to network.

- Use the Internet and conduct a search looking for companies providing similar services.

- Use the want ads in the newspaper and industry magazines. These are a great source of information about small companies.

- Read current trade publications.

- Do a combination of the above.

Remember not to use market research as an excuse not to begin selling your product or service.

Establishing marketing objectives

Based on your unique selling proposition and your vision, you need to create marketing objectives for your business. More detail on the criteria for effective objectives is included in Chapter 4.

These objectives need to meet **SMART** criteria.

S – Specific
M – Measurable
A – Aligned
R – Results-oriented
T – Time-based.

There is normally a variety of marketing objectives for a consulting business under several categories:

- share of the market
- market penetration
- market visibility
- size of database

- number of newsletters.

Make sure you set specific objectives for your marketing plan – what is not measured, does not get done! (For example: To establish a database of 200 contacts by 31 December, 200X.) If you don't know where you're going, you'll probably end up somewhere else.

The reason for setting specific objectives is to have a target to work towards. It is always better to have an objective. If you don't reach that objective, it is easy to change it and work towards reaching it in the future. If you don't start with an objective you have no way of knowing whether you've reached it or not.

Segmenting the market
Segmenting the market involves breaking down the market into smaller sub-sections. The benefit of segmenting the market is that you can then target marketing efforts more effectively. The segmentation can be made by:

- industry, such as retail, software, hardware, wholesale, tele-communications, non-profit
- geographical area, such as England, UK, Europe, USA
- company size, such as small (under 100 people), medium, large
- maturity of company: start-up, mature
- type of company culture
- functional category, such as human resources, web page design, training, marketing
- functional speciality within functional category; for example, within human resources there are the functional specialities of payroll, compensation, benefits and recruiting.

For example, you may wish to provide leadership training and development services to small-size companies in the London area, concentrating on classroom presentation and curriculum development.

Defining your product or service
This stage in the marketing process involves defining the services you offer in terms of **features** and **benefits**.

The **features** of a product or service include **facts** about the product, its **function** information about the product, its characteristics, and its design or construction. Customers usually buy features only when they relate to benefits.

A **benefit** is anything that contributes to an improvement in condition, produces an advantage, or aids in accomplishing a task. It is the **positive result** or **bonus** achieved as a result of using your product or service. It shows how a company will gain from using these services, what the services can do, and what the bottom line is. It answers the questions 'What's in it for me?' or 'What's in it for my company?'

It is critical to define your product or service in user-friendly terms through the use of features and benefits, specifically in relation to how they **meet business needs**. Customers are interested in benefits, but we are often most comfortable talking about features. A benefit answers the questions:

Who cares?
So what?

A transition statement to link the feature to the benefit is:

Which means that...

Benefits can be **tangible** (the benefit can be measured objectively) or **intangible**. Benefits combined create the **ultimate benefit**, which is the overall benefit of the product or service to the individual or organisation.

Figure 14 gives examples of the features and benefits of a table. This is a tangible product to demonstrate how this process works.

Feature	Who cares? So what?	Which means that	Benefit	Ultimate benefit
Four legs	Who cares? So what?	Which means that....	The table has stability (tangible)	Efficient working space
Brown	Who cares? So what?	Which means that....	The table is aesthetically pleasing (intangible)	
14 square feet of surface area	Who cares? So what?	Which means that...	It is spacious and holds a lot of material (tangible)	

Fig. 14. Features and benefits of a table.

It is harder to think about a **service** in terms of features and benefits because a service itself is intangible, and varies from one moment to another. It also varies according to the customer's mood at any one time. Describing a service such as consulting differs considerably from describing a product such as a car. A car is manufactured in one location and then delivered for sale to the customer in another. A service is often created and delivered simultaneously. As a result of conducting a consulting project, you concurrently deliver it. Goods are produced; services are performed.

These differences pose a special challenge to consultants. How do you make relatively invisible services seem real and useful to prospective clients? This is achieved by making sure the services are understood, and by somehow making them more tangible using features and benefits.

It is also harder to think about a service without a specific customer in mind because most services will be designed and delivered to meet a specific customer's needs. However, the mental exercise of differentiating between the features and benefits of your consulting service will help you in the sales interaction, as well as when you are creating marketing collateral for yourself, which is discussed later in this chapter.

Let's look at one example of features and benefits for a service: an eight-hour training programme on consulting and making money at it – see Figure 15.

Consulting and making money at it (service):				
Feature	Who cares? So what?	Which means that...	Benefit	Ultimate benefit
One-day programme	Who cares? So what?	Which means that...	Time effective (tangible)	Successful consulting business
Learn marketing strategies	Who cares? So what?	Which means that...	Increase exposure (intangible) Get clients (tangible)	
Participant materials are supplied as a reference tool	Who cares? So what?	Which means that...	Greater retention (intangible)	
Interactive with exercises and discussion	Who cares? So what?	Which means that...	Greater learning (tangible)	

Fig. 15. Features and benefits of a service.

Based on the features and benefits you outlined for your product/service and the market research you have conducted, fill in the chart in Figure 16 with your own products/services, their features and benefits, and how they fulfil business needs. Remember that companies buy benefits even though we are most comfortable selling features, and if you offer too many features, you may actually deter the sale by making the customer feel inadequate. Benefits are more important to the client than features. Sometimes it is not necessary to even discuss features, only benefits.

Your services				
Feature	Who cares? So what?	Which means that...	Benefit	Ultimate benefit
	Who cares? So what?	Which means that...		
	Who cares? So what?	Which means that...		
	Who cares? So what?	Which means that...		
	Who cares? So what?	Which means that...		

Fig. 16. Features and benefits – form.

Deciding your promotional plan

Once you have identified your potential clients and clarified your marketing plan, you need to determine the most appropriate promotional strategies for acquiring clients. All too often, consultants randomly select marketing tools. They might hand out brochures, give speeches and make personal calls. However, these consultants often can't explain why they selected these tools over others. They have not targeted their clients nor defined their message adequately.

Your promotional plan should include some or all of the following:

- advertising
- public relations
- giving speeches
- marketing communications
- newsletters and mailings
- trade shows and exhibitions
- web page.

More detail on promotional strategies will be included in the next section of this chapter.

Creating a schedule

As a consultant, it is important to plan your marketing strategy. Often time taken in this area directly detracts from time spent in the most critical part of the consulting process: actually talking to and influencing clients. There are many prospective consultants who have great brochures and no customers!

A schedule needs to include:

- plans for market research
- times to set objectives
- schedules for defining products and services
- promotional campaign defined according to what and when.

If you know to whom, why, what and how you plan to market, then you must only decide when. Your timing should consider three factors:

1. When the client is most receptive.

2. When the client is least likely to receive competitors' messages.

3. When your resources will permit you both to market and to meet the demand created by marketing.

USING PROMOTIONAL STRATEGIES

The purpose of promotional strategies is to create leads for, and awareness of, your consulting business. As you can see from the funnel shown in Chapter 6 (Figure 18), promotional activity helps to raise awareness and create interest, but does not confirm a need. **Only when your business is established will promotional activities directly produce revenue.** Remember not to use undertaking promotional strategies as an excuse for not calling or meeting with clients!

Promotion is necessary therefore to:

- begin the process of obtaining new clients

- raise interest in your product or service

- increase awareness of your business

- establish or modify your image

- educate the public through your efforts

- attract new employees

- provide a public service.

Let's review ideas and strategies within each of the key categories (see Figure 17).

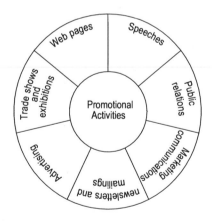

Fig. 17. Promotional activities.

Advertising

Advertising is used to raise awareness and promote interest in a product or service. Advertising results are hard to quantify, and the advertising needs to be regular to obtain any benefits. When starting your consulting business, if advertising is used at all, it needs to be extremely selective and focused on the particular market segment or industry segment where your consulting provides value. Depending on your functional expertise, you may want to consider the following possibilities:

- *Yellow Pages*
- local newspapers
- trade directory
- conference publications
- exhibition catalogues
- local association newsletters.

All the above can be expensive. They also might not directly bring in business, but they will raise an awareness of you and what you are doing.

Trade shows and exhibitions
In the early stages of your business, trade shows can appear to be an expensive investment. However, it is always possible to attend trade shows:

- as a delegate in a professional development activity
- to build a network
- to conduct market research
- to identify possible strategic alliances
- to raise awareness by advertising in trade show guides
- to get information on competition.

Web pages
As Internet use continues to grow, web-based marketing activities will become more critical to new business development. Some organisations have eliminated conventional marketing channels and replaced them with web-based sales and distribution. Other organisations use web-based marketing to supplement their marketing efforts.

Advantages
- Inexpensive promotional channel.
- Reaches a wide range of audiences.
- Easy and quick to put together and change.
- Requires minimal technical expertise.
- Can offer web site information to people who inquire and provides a quicker access to data.

Disadvantages
- No personal recommendation – you will have to meet with any prospective organisation.
- Huge, possibly causing your product/service to get lost.
- Many unqualified leads are time-consuming.
- Better used as a support to existing customers and prospects than to generate a business.

Giving speeches
Speeches are frequently used to familiarise clients with a consultant's capabilities. Of course your topic must be timely and your presentation professional.

Advantages
- Gives you credibility within a specific subject area.
- Allows you personally to demonstrate your verbal capability.

Disadvantages
- Time-consuming. One hour's presentation takes eight hours of preparation.
- Free speeches may generate . . . lots more free speeches!
- Giving free speeches places your product in the 'free' category.

Public relations
Public relations is often viewed as unpaid advertising. It means that your business gains exposure in trade publications without a monetary payment from you, and as a result carries more credibility.

Public relations includes publishing articles and books, submitting articles, being quoted in the business press, undertaking a formal public relations campaign such as issuing press releases, targeting specific journalists, and obtaining local radio or TV exposure. Published articles and books can establish and enhance both your image and your reputation, particularly if you have a specific story to tell within your area of expertise. There are many trade publications, most of which actively seek material. Again you should write for journals whose readers can use your services. Be aware, however, that writing is very time-consuming and it is hard to guarantee or quantify results.

The area of public relations can be very effective, but time-consuming, with no controlled output.

Advantages
- 'Unpaid advertising'.

- More credibility than 'paid advertising'.

- Greater market awareness.

Disadvantages
- Writing is very time-consuming.

- No guaranteed results.

- Great strategy to avoid talking to 'real people'.

Marketing communications
Marketing communications encompass brochures, business cards and cover letters.

Brochures
With the availability of desktop publishing, it has become easier to avoid the high costs of producing brochures. In the early stages of consulting, a professionally produced summary of qualifications in the form of a CV is adequate. Clients expect brochures but most often as a back-up device. Remember that people buy people – *not* paper. Make sure your brochure lists **benefits** as well as **features**.

Business cards
Business cards are an essential part of building the corporate identity of your business. However, they are a tool best used face-to-face, so again do not use creating a business card as an excuse for not talking to prospective customers. Use of business cards varies from culture to culture, so make sure you familiarise yourself with local customs when you are travelling to a new country.

Cover letters

Cover letters support your brochure and/or proposal when marketing your services. They need to be personally written for each client, addressing specific issues regarding that client's needs and the way you can meet those needs. (Proposals will be discussed in detail in the next chapter.)

Newsletters and mailings

If you have unique information to share, or wish to keep in contact with those on your database when you are busy, newsletters are an effective communications tool. In addition, if you index your database you can then mail articles you read on specific topics to target audiences. For example, if some of your customers are interested in customer service, you could mail them an interesting customer service article you have read with a brief note attached to it.

ESTABLISHING YOUR NETWORK

Your network is your prime business development and maintenance tool. Referrals by past or present clients are the most commonly used means of obtaining new business. A survey made by the Institute of Management Consultants suggests that repeat business constitutes 70 per cent of all business while referrals make up 15 per cent. Networking is very important for marketing yourself, particularly in the early stages. Here are a few guidelines for establishing and formalising your network.

Building the network

Your network should number approximately 200 people. It will be a dynamic, constantly changing promotional tool that must be kept current. You can expect your database to turn over approximately 25 per cent (and up to 50 per cent) per annum.

Although this sounds like a large number of people, you create a network by identifying all the people you know (your primary contacts) as well as your secondary contacts (those people you have been referred to). Your network comes from:

- friends

- family

- colleagues, past and present

- university alumni associations
- trade organisations
- neighbours
- the pub
- sports clubs
- people you meet when travelling
- prospects from presentations
- contacts from exhibitions and conferences
- vendors/suppliers from previous jobs.

The only **criteria** are:
- You personally know the person.
- You respect the person.
- Those on the list would probably like to hear from you.
- You ensure that there is a mutual exchange of benefits/ information.
- The person you contact would remember you, e.g. you probably have met him or her more than once.

This way you ensure that you are not acting like the 'networking barracuda' who appears always to have something to sell and whom people avoid like the plague!

It is impossible to talk to 200 people often, so you might want to use one or more of the following to stay in touch:

- newsletter
- e-mail
- Christmas card/letter.

Putting the network on an electronic database

The database ideally should have an individual's name, company name, job title, phone number, fax number, e-mail address, and some sort of contact information. It is critical to record your network on some type of database/sales management tool such as ACT^{TM}, $Access^{TM}$, etc., not on a $Rolodex^{TM}$ or business cards. The benefits of this are:

- easy access for mailing and newsletters
- centrally available
- convenient to update
- ability to sort by category.

The network can then be classified into different categories such as:

- **General contacts**. The world at large.

- **Suspects**. Suspects are prequalified in some way. They probably won't give you business, but know someone who might. They are influencers and should compose about 25 per cent of your network. (See Chapter 6 for more information.)

- **Prospects**. These are people with a defined need. (See Chapter 6 for more information.)

- **Clients**. These are people for whom you have done work during the past year. There should be from ten to 20 names on this list.

- **Key clients**. The two to five people you are currently doing work for. This makes up the largest part of your current revenue.

- **Interest in a specific area**. Teams, consulting.

More information on categorising your network is included in Chapter 6. The database will need to be updated at least once a month with new contacts. Now that you have established your marketing direction, you will need to move on to the critical 'make or break' element of running a successful consulting business: selling your services. But first take a few moments to review the checklist, case studies and action points.

CHECKLIST

1. Have you conducted initial market research into your area of expertise?

2. Have you established three clear marketing objectives?

3. Have you defined clearly the business needs your product and service address?

4. Have you identified three competitors and defined how you differ from them?

5. Have you analysed market segments and defined three markets for your business service?

6. Have you prioritised your promotional activity and established a promotional plan for the next three months?

7. Have you created a list of 200 people?

8. Have you bought a database program to track your database activities?

CASE STUDIES

Marie is an enthusiastic marketer

Marie has spent some time in marketing in a previous job, and so has already completed much of her marketing planning. Because her industry is highly dispersed, she has decided to conduct informal market research by talking to people she knows who are both consultants and possible clients. She has created a list of 30 people, whom she plans to talk to in the next three weeks. Her main purpose in these calls is to determine market interest for her product and service, and to understand current market rates. Her marketing objectives are to obtain two more clients within the next six months and to establish a database of over 200 names on Access^{TM}.

While she is aware of the other promotional activities, because of her gregarious nature and verbal fluency, she plans to rely primarily on the telephone and face-to-face meetings to build her business. She is going to barter with a friend of hers to help her create a web page in exchange for providing him with some leads for possible web page development. She has already established over 100 names on her database, categorised according to their likelihood of directly bringing in business, and is feeling positive about business opportunities.

Frank is using his expertise to build business

Using the web, Frank has conducted market research into other consultants who provide services, and into the market in general for call centre process improvement. Based on this analysis, he believes his business will be viable.

He uses e-mail to initiate contacts with the people he finds on the web and is planning to establish strategic partnerships with local ISO 9001 certification organisations as an additional resource. He has created his own web page to describe his capabilities. He has

Frank's services – review of operational effectiveness				
Feature	Who cares? So what?	Which means that...	Benefit	Ultimate benefit
Call flow and handling analysis	Who cares? So what?	Which means that..	Improve productivity in call flow	Increased customer satisfaction
Problem handling and resolution	Who cares? So what?	Which means that...	Quicker problem resolution time	
Internal and external customer service level agreements	Who cares? So what?	Which means that...	Increased efficiency	
Complete process flow analysis	Who cares? So what?	Which means that..	Improved process flow	
Complete measurement and reporting	Who cares? So what?	Which means that...	Enable continuous improvement	
People: staff skill analysis and recommendations	Who cares? So what?	Which means that...	Greater employee retention	
Tools and technologies assessment and improvement recommendations	Who cares? So what?	Which means that...	Increased contribution margin	

linked his web page to other call centre services to facilitate prospects finding him.

He is continuing his teaching at the community college, both as a way to enhance his credibility, and as a source for possible new business. He is investigating costs for advertising in local and national computer magazines and/or small business/entrepreneur magazines. He is going to attend a Help Desk Managers conference and is considering placing an advertisement in the conference publication. In addition, he has bought an e-mail distribution list and he plans to e-mail an attachment describing his services. He is considering creating a CD-ROM describing his expertise and services to send to those who reply.

He has created an e-mail list of friends and colleagues and plans to send them the attachment describing his services. He is planning to cover his initial start-up time with a contract from his existing organisation.

Linda is uncomfortable 'getting out there'

Linda wants to make sure she is fully prepared before she talks to any of her contacts. She has created a brochure and business cards, and has attended a workshop to help her with ideas on how to get started. She has decided to conduct formalised market research and to this end has created a questionnaire, and has begun to collate a mailing list. She plans to wait until the questionnaires are returned, and she has summarised the data before she contacts anyone, because she does not want to appear ignorant. She is unsure about undertaking promotional efforts, and believes that her expertise is sufficient to find business. One or two people have said she should call them when she is 'ready', as they might be able to help her. She is considering doing a mailer and then waiting for people to call her. She is uncomfortable making what she perceives to be cold calls and believes that if she is good enough, business will come to her.

ACTION POINTS

1. In terms of your marketing plan, what do you consider to be the market for your product or service? How comfortable are you establishing marketing objectives and what segments do you wish to concentrate on initially?

2. What promotional strategies are best for your business? What are the personal challenges you face in defining and deciding to use these strategies? What time commitment will you allocate to your promotional efforts?

3. What size network will you need to be able to facilitate your business growth? What are your personal reservations about contacting people you know for advice and how will you address these concerns? How will you categorise your database and ensure you are focusing on those people who will help to grow your business, not just those you like?

6

Selling Your Service

The most challenging part of consulting is finding clients. This process is often referred to as business development. Marketing looks at the big picture of informing the public of your services. Selling is a specific marketing activity that results in a consulting assignment. Selling usually takes place in a face-to-face setting. But there is no mistake about it: consultants must sell their services in the same way as anyone else. The difference between successful and unsuccessful consultants is usually their ability to sell.

OVERCOMING YOUR FEAR OF SELLING

Often we view selling as a game in which one side wins and one side loses. When we hear the word 'sell', often the first thing that comes to mind is:

- used car salesmen
- pushy tactics
- telephone marketing calls at night
- unsolicited products or services
- products that don't meet needs.

Instead of thinking about **selling** to your customers, change two letters and think about **helping** them instead. When you provide a service to clients, you will be helping them meet a business need, solve a problem and/or achieve a business objective. If you cannot help them, then don't sell to them!

Selling at its best is a mutually satisfying interaction in which both sides win. On the one hand, the client's needs are met. On the other hand, the consultant generates income, engages in his or her profession, and reaps personal rewards for helping the client. In addition, selling yourself can be simpler than selling a product – you know what you can do. But it can also be more difficult because a refusal can be viewed as a personal rejection.

To overcome a fear of selling, follow these three steps:

1. Realise why selling is in your best interest.
2. Understand the emotional response behind your fears.
3. Learn the skills that enable you to sell successfully.

THE SALES PROCESS

The sales process (see Figure 18) shows the steps that are involved in obtaining clients and normally runs from the time you begin marketing to the time you close the deal.

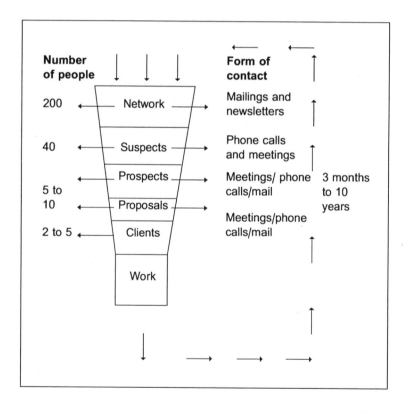

Fig. 18. The sales process.

Your network

As you read in Chapter 5, your network is the key building block for your business. From this base of about 200 people, you will probably generate 95 per cent of your new business opportunities. However, you will not be able to talk to or meet with this number of people on a regular basis, so tools such as your newsletter, mailing and cards are critical for maintaining contact with your database. If you tried to contact this network personally, you would become submerged in returning phone calls and meeting people, and would be unable to focus on the key individuals who can help you grow your business.

Suspects

A category within your database is those individuals whom you class as suspects. Suspects normally make up about 20–25 per cent of your database, or approximately 40–50 people. Suspects can fit into the following categories:

- those who are pre-qualified in some way
- those who are influential in the industry
- other consultants whom you might use for work and who also might require your services
- those who are decision-makers in their area
- brokers in the industry you are in
- leading-edge thinkers
- those who possess some type of unique content knowledge.

These individuals do not have a defined need as yet, but they are the contacts from whom future business is likely to arise. Suspects are normally contacted by phone, with some face-to-face meetings. Focusing energy in this area will stimulate other, more concrete business opportunities.

Prospects

Prospective leads have the ability to buy, the right to buy and the need to buy, often within a short time period. Your sales funnel at any one time will have between five and ten prospects depending on the size and maturity of your business. Your prospects come from two sources: your marketing efforts and your personal contact system (suspects and network).

Earlier we looked at promotional strategies and your network. In this chapter we will spend more time on skills and techniques in the personal selling arena. Most of the interaction with prospects is conducted in face-to-face meetings, where needs are clearly identified and the correct solution for the prospective client defined. There may be two to three meetings as the prospect's needs are refined and the sales process continues towards its conclusion.

Proposals

Proposals are normally the final part of the sales process where you document the information and approach you have discussed with the prospect. The proposal should be a formal summary of the discussions and is the final critical step in closing the business. Too often, however, consultants send 'standard proposals' where the prospect has not been prequalified, resulting in a waste of time and paper. At any one time, you will probably have two to three proposals outstanding.

Clients

If you are successful in clearly defining the client requirements, often the prospect will become a client. At any one time, a consulting business probably needs between five and ten clients. If the business only has one client, then it may be exposed if there is a sudden change in the client's strategy. For example, a training company had 90 per cent of its business with Esso. When there were some major changes in the oil industry, they had to completely rebuild their business. If the organisation has too many clients, then the consultant may become overwhelmed and give less than top-quality service to all clients.

Recycling the funnel

Clients often then become prospects for more business, provide leads and become part of the network once again, and as a result are 'recycled' through the funnel.

If this process is working effectively the time taken to close business may be as little as three months. The sales cycle is definitely shortening as the rate of change in the world increases. However, there is normally a time delay between when you originally make contact and when you begin to find solid prospects. Part of the reason for having a sufficient amount of money to cover expenses for six months is to protect yourself from the length of the sales cycle. More detail on this is included in Chapter 7.

Planning for sales

The amount of time spent selling depends on the type of consulting and the duration of the average consulting contract. The important thing is to make sure there are a certain number of clients in the pipeline at any one time. You need to consider:

- what size of network you need
- how many calls are needed to secure a meeting
- how many meetings are needed to submit a proposal
- how many proposals are needed to close one client
- how long each client takes to close.

These sales activities usually take place in sequence. Phone calls lead to meetings, meetings lead to proposals, proposals lead to work.

ESTABLISHING SALES OBJECTIVES

Without a selling orientation you can easily overlook activities necessary for the continuation of your consulting practice. By paying attention to the sales process, you can prevent the nightmare of running out of consulting projects and avoid the feast or famine syndrome. In any time period you need to ensure that you have clearly stated, measurable sales objectives for each step in the sales process; in other words, that you are talking to suspects, meeting with prospects and writing proposals. These objectives need to meet **SMART** criteria as outlined in Chapter 4.

S – Specific
M – Measurable
A – Aligned
R – Results-oriented
T – Time-based

There is normally a variety of sales objectives for a consulting business under several categories:

- target clients
- number of clients per year
- average reorder value

- number of new clients per year
- number of suspects and targets for frequency of contact
- number of prospects and targets for frequency of contact
- number of proposals per month
- number of meetings per week
- number of telephone calls per week.

TELEPHONE MARKETING

Selling, developing and delivering a service such as consulting differs considerably from selling a product like a car. These differences pose a special challenge to consultants. How do you make relatively invisible services seem real and useful to prospective clients? This is achieved by making sure the services are understood, and by somehow making them more tangible by talking to and meeting with suspects and prospects.

Marketing by telephone is not the same as cold calling. Marketing by telephone involves calling people from your network suspect and prospect lists to obtain ideas and information. If you are effective with contacting people you know, you will never need to make a cold call.

Advantages and disadvantages of telephone marketing

Advantages
- Saves time. You can cover many people in a short time. The telephone is an incredibly time-effective tool, particularly in the early stages of business development.

- Saves money. Costs less than travelling to face-to-face meetings.

Disadvantages
- No face-to-face contact. You are not able to see body language cues and therefore it can be harder to build rapport.

- Difficulty in contact. It is becoming increasingly difficult to talk to 'live' people, instead of message machines.

Telephone marketing requires a concentrated, focused environment, plus rapid evaluation and decision-making. But the benefits can be considerable in terms of increased business.

General guidelines for telephone marketing

- 'Chunk' your time: plan for at least two hours of telephone calls three times a week in the set-up stages of your business, and at least two, three-hour sessions per week when your business is established.

- Make sure you utilise your body clock effectively. Telephone marketing is hard work, so make sure if you are a 'lark' (best in the morning) that you make phone calls then. If you are an 'owl' (best in the afternoon and evening), make phone calls then.

- If you are organised, you can make 30–45 calls in a two to three-hour time frame.

- Most of the time (approximately 75 per cent) you will be leaving messages or voicemails. Make sure you leave a specific message including your name and number, the reason you called, and a good time to call back.

- If you are leaving a message on a voicemail, state your name and number at the beginning of the call, and then repeat it again at the end.

- Don't rush when you repeat your phone number!

- Even if you have known the person for a long time, always leave your number. You never know if they have lost their organiser, or if their system has crashed!

- Make at least three to five phone calls to the same person without giving up. Research conducted of a sales force showed that the women were more successful than the men in the group because they made more calls than the men did, and many of the decisions to buy took place on the fifth call. Often we take it personally when people do not call us back. Most of the time they are simply busy, not ignoring us!

- If the person still does not return your call, you could send a letter with information and wait for him or her to contact you.

- Call back every three to five days. On average people return the call, if they are going to, within two to three days.

- The ideal use of the telephone in marketing your business would be to make the initial call, send information, and then call again after the information has been received and enough time has passed for the recipient to have read it. This normally doubles the success rate.

Preparing for making telephone calls

As with most work time spent in preparing and planning can save time when actually making calls. Here are some **pre-call planning ideas** to help you prepare for making contact on the phone:

- Create a mental picture of who you are contacting and what you both want to accomplish as a result of this phone call.

- What do you know about this contact, his or her company and background?

- What is your objective in calling?

- What questions are you going to ask?

- How did you obtain the name of this contact?

- What specific questions may this contact ask, based on your knowledge of him or her?

- Do you understand every conceivable aspect of your background that may be relevant?

- Make sure your voice is pleasant and upbeat.

- Monitor your voice in terms of pitch/tone, accent, volume and inflections.

- Be sincere.

In addition, you need to **prepare your purpose and story** for your contacts. A simple model for preparing your purpose and story is to go through four specific sections. This should take from 30 seconds to two minutes to deliver. Any longer than that and people will not listen. The four steps are as follows:

1. Your **personal** background and/or your connection to the person.

2. Your **educational** background, particularly if this will enhance your credibility.

3. Your **business** background: a few summary statements providing your key areas of expertise and unique selling proposition.

4. The bridge connecting what you are doing as a consultant and what help or advice you are looking for from him or her.

Example

1. *Personal.* Hi. My name is...and we met at the...meeting last week where you asked me to follow up with you this week.

2. *Educational background.* I have a Masters in Organisational Development from...

3. *Business background.* As you know, I am a training consultant with over 20 years of experience in the training and organisational development industry. For the past four years I have been running my own business, and my expertise includes assessing training needs, developing and delivering training solutions, and training internal trainers. The value I could bring to your organisation (my unique selling proposition) is that I am a businessperson first and a trainer second, which means that any training solutions I offer are practical and business-results focused.

4. *Bridge.* And the reason I am calling today is...

Take a moment now and create your purpose and story:

_____

_____

_____

_____

Managing the telephone interaction

Initially you will want to decide what sort of help or ideas you need from your network. Always identify the purpose of your call. It can be to:

- gather advice
- fix a meeting
- qualify a lead
- obtain other names
- follow up on a proposal, etc.

You will generally contact them by telephone so you need to sound confident, organised and prepared. This will help to make your contacts feel comfortable helping you.

Figures 19, 20 and 21 set out the steps in the telephone interaction in a variety of situations: when the person is there and it is a good time, when it is not a good time, and when there is a voicemail.

Step in the call	Person is there: good time
1. Identify purpose for call: • to generate a meeting	
2. Short introduction	Hello, this is... We met at the recent Help Desk Institute Meeting and you suggested I call you about process re-engineering. (Personal information)
3. Ask for permission	Is this a good time? (Yes)
4. Introduce purpose and story (30 seconds to two minutes maximum!)	I have a Masters Degree in Quality Engineering. (Education) I have spent the last 20 years both in the field and at corporate headquarters managing and directing technical support operations, working for such organisations as Amdahl, Oracle and IBM. The specific expertise I bring is that I combine both strategy and process improvement experience, with a practical implementation focus. (Business background) The reason I am calling today is because we discussed the process re-engineering project you are undertaking and thought I might be able to help. (Bridge/transition)
5. Transition into questions	What was the driving force behind your process engineering? How far are you into the process? What are the results so far? How far are you meeting expectations? What is working? Etc.
6. Listen to answers	Make notes to act as the basis for more questions. After a two-way discussion lasting approximately 3–4 minutes, transition.
7. Transition	It seems like we might have a fit in terms of your needs and the services I could provide.
8. Date for a meeting	I will be in your area on ..Is there any time that day that would work for you? (Pick any date within the next two weeks that you are available. Although you may not have a trip planned to that area, you will if they agree to meet with you!)

Fig. 19. Telephone interaction – person is there and it's a good time.

Step in the Call	Person is there: not a good time
1. Identify purpose for call: ● to ask for advice/information	
2. Short introduction with purpose	Hello, this is... We worked together at Sun when you were the CFO and I was the AP Manager. I was calling to see if you could give me any advice since I'm setting up my own consulting business. (Personal information)
3. Ask for permission	Is this a good time? (No)
4. Not a good time	When would you like me to try again?
5. Confirm time	So I will call you back at...
6. Finish call	Thank you and I will look forward to catching up personally then.
7. Call back when promised	If there: continue with purpose, story, questions and summary. If the person is not there, they now have an informal obligation to call you back because you made an appointment and they broke it.
8. Call back three days later if don't hear, and start again	

Fig. 20. Telephone interaction – person is there and it's not a good time.

Depending on the purpose of your call, you will use different transitions or bridges. In Figure 20, if the person had been there, you could have asked the following bridge and questions:

Bridge (to ask for names and advice). If you were in my situation, whom would you talk to? What would you do? Who else might have ideas?

If you do talk to someone, be sure to send a thank you note if the person has given you good, useful advice or if he or she has given you a lead. You want to be comfortable calling again if necessary.

Step in the call	Person is not there: voicemail
1. Identify purpose for call: ● to qualify prospects	
2. Short introduction	Hello, this is... Julie suggested I call you regarding sales training for your organisation.
3. Introduce purpose and story (30 seconds to two minutes maximum)	I have a Masters Degree in Organisational Development. (Educational) I recently left... organisation where I was responsible for rolling out sales training to over 5,000 associates in a three month period resulting in a 17 per cent increase in comparative store sales. (Business background) The reason I am calling today is because Julie suggested you might need help in training associates at your stores. (Bridge/transition)
4. Transition into call back	I would be very interested in talking to you about your current sales training process, to discover in what areas I may be able to help you.
5. Give availability	I will be available tomorrow and Friday.
6. Restate contact information	Again, my name is... and my phone number is... I look forward to talking to you personally soon.

Fig. 21. Telephone interaction – person is not there and you get voicemail.

Optimising telephone contact

Some other ideas to optimise telephone contact include the following:

- Limit your own talking.
- Turn off your own feelings.
- Concentrate.
- Think as if you were the other person.

- Ask questions.
- Don't interrupt.
- Listen for ideas, not just words.
- React to ideas.
- Listen for overtones.
- Use interjections.
- Take notes.

As you can see, managing the telephone interaction is critical to optimising your business success. However, many people feel uncomfortable about contacting others for information or for ideas. By being clear about your purpose and examining reasons for your reluctance, you can overcome this obstacle. JUST DO IT!

Now let's look at skills and techniques for the face-to-face interaction with prospective clients.

MANAGING THE SALES MEETING
Using LAURA
Use the following technique to help you **remember names**:

L – Look at the person and get a mental picture *first*.
A – Ask the name.
U – Understand the name, how is it pronounced, where is it from, etc.
R – Repeat the name once or twice.
A – Associate the name, e.g. other people with that name, location, etc.

Adapting to different temperaments
Each temperament communicates in a different way and brings different business benefits. Make sure you adapt your style and word choice to different customers.

- **Guardians** will be more deliberate in their approach and will want detailed, sequential information. The benefits they buy are concrete, bottom-line savings of time/money, and process improvements.

- **Artisans** will be quicker moving and talking and will want to 'get to the point'. The benefits they buy are quick, easy services that will make an impact on business performance.

- **Rationals** will be objective and talk about strategies, concepts and models. The benefits they buy are new operating approaches that improve business positioning.

- **Idealists** will be empathetic and talk about the purpose and meaning of services. The benefits they buy are ability to develop and optimise potential, integrated with overall company direction.

Remembering SELL

Keep in mind the following acronym to help you with managing the face-to-face sales meeting:

S – Start the interaction.
E – Engage the client: ask open-ended questions, listen, and paraphrase.
L – List features and benefits that relate to the client's needs.
L – Leave with the next step planned.

Let's look at these steps in a little more detail.

S: Start the interaction

This stage involves establishing rapport with the client and will last anywhere from a few moments to over ten minutes based on the person's style. The need for this step is greater in the early stages of the consulting relationship. A prospective client won't buy from someone he or she doesn't like.

The step includes shaking hands and exchanging business cards. When you meet the prospect for the first time, remember that you communicate primarily through body language (55 per cent) and the way you say the words (38 per cent). The word choice is nowhere near as important as the delivery and overall look. In this stage you can talk about common interests, conduct small talk about business or discuss something about the company.

You will know when the client is ready to move on to the next step of the interaction because he or she will normally change posture: pick up a pen, sit forward, or move somehow. It is critical that you catch this clue because you then need to move into the next step of the sales meeting, which is engaging the client. If you miss this clue and the prospective client asks you to describe your services you will not know the specific needs the client wishes to be addressed.

E: Engage the client

The critical point in selling a service is to identify client needs and objectives before you begin to describe your products or services. Customers will only commit to purchasing services when they are convinced the consultant's support will help them meet their business objectives. The chances for closing a sale are greater if you actively search out the customer's needs. But more importantly, customers will feel more valued if the consultant takes an active interest in their needs.

There are two ways of uncovering customer needs: making assumptions, and asking questions.

- **Making assumptions** is risky.

- **Asking questions** should mean primarily open-ended questions. Open-ended questions cannot be answered by 'yes' or 'no'.

Asking open-ended questions
This part of the sales interaction can last over 20 minutes and requires asking extensive open-ended questions about the client's current business situation, overall business objectives and specific challenges in the area where you can provide help. Use who, what, when, where, why and how to begin open-ended questions. Phrases such as 'tell me about...', 'describe...' and 'explain...' act as excellent topic-opener statements to begin a subject area. The questions will normally start from the general level, in terms of business challenges, and become more specific, focusing on the areas in which you can provide a service. In the Appendix is a general list of questions that can be used to gather information about the business.

Listening actively
Ask open-ended questions, take notes, and be an active listener. Don't be afraid of silence after asking open-ended questions. On average the person may stop and reflect for between four and ten seconds. In western society we are often uncomfortable with silence and fill it by answering our own questions. If you do this, you will lose control of the interaction and not gather enough information about client needs. You need to ensure that you give the person time to think and talk, then paraphrase what they have said.

Listening is a very complex skill. Too often we find ourselves 'rehearsing' (thinking about what *we* are going to say), or jumping too early to conclusions rather than listening. Paying attention to the customer, processing what they have said (thinking about it from their perspective) and paraphrasing can help fine-tune your listening skills.

Paraphrasing
Paraphrasing is repeating back to the customer in your own words, what he or she has just told you. Paraphrasing has many benefits, which include:

- validating the customer

- checking for understanding between what you heard and what they said

- giving you time to think about the next questions you wish to ask.

Probing for specifics
You probe for specifics when you ask for more specific information within a subject area. For example, 'You said you introduced sales training over two years ago with limited success. Tell me more about the content of that training programme and the methodology you used to introduce it.'

You will know when you have asked too many questions because the prospective client's posture will change. This is the time to begin to describe the products and services you can offer that will meet their needs. You don't want them to ask you what you do – that means you've gone on too long asking questions and have lost their interest.

L: List features and benefits that relate to the client's needs

List features relating to client needs
At this point in the selling process you need to explain the services you offer in terms of the features and benefits you determined in Chapter 5. The benefits will relate directly to the needs you have identified in the sales meeting.

This is the step in the sales interaction when the business can be sold or lost. Many consultants fail to watch the body language clues from the client as they describe their service's features and benefits. As a result they continue to talk and walk straight into and out of the sale. If you miss that critical moment when the client wishes to buy, then you may not be able to close the sale. Over half of sales are lost because the critical cues from the customer are missed.

Asking for status
If you are not sure where you are in the process, the best thing you can do is to ask the client. If you see a change of posture ask one of the following four questions:

- How does that sound?

- How does this information look?

- What do you think?

- How do you feel about this information?

If they tell you they are interested, then this gives you a chance to move to the next step. If this is not adequate, you can acknowledge the concern and then move back through the process of engaging the customer by asking more open-ended questions, listening and paraphrasing. Then the same questions can be repeated.

L: Leave with the next step planned
Often the end of the interaction does not mean the closing of the sale. When selling services, it takes on average two to three appointments to close the sale. However, it is necessary to ensure that when you leave, you have the critical next steps identified so that you do not have to revisit the voicemail endless cycle! The next steps could include:

- a further meeting with other decision-makers and influencers

- sending a proposal

- a formal presentation to senior management.

Part of this process involves anticipating objections. If the sales process has been followed effectively, then objections will have been addressed in the objectives, features and benefits section.

Figure 22 summarises the critical steps, skills and techniques in managing the sales meeting.

WRITING SUCCESSFUL PROPOSALS
Many appointments result in a client's request for a proposal. A proposal is usually a document you write for the client that:

Step in the sales meeting	Skills and techniques
S: Start the interaction (2 – 10 minutes)	• Use positive body language • Be aware of body language • Talk about business environment • Find common interests • Watch for changes in posture • Ask open-ended questions
E: Engage the client (20 minutes)	• Listen actively • Probe for specifics • Paraphrase • Watch for changes in posture
L: List features and benefits (20 minutes)	• Link benefits to needs • Watch for changes in posture • Ask for status: How does that sound? Look? Feel? What do you think? • Repeat concern • Ask questions, listen, paraphrase and probe • Restate features and benefits • Ask again for status
L: Leave with the next step planned (2 – 10 minutes)	• Meeting • Proposal • Presentation • Contract • Start date

Fig. 22. Sales meeting: SELL.

• describes your understanding of the client's need

• paraphrases the key information gathered in the meeting(s) with the client and restates what the client requested

• states what you intend to do for the client

• indicates what anticipated results and potential benefits the client will gain as a consequence of the engagement

• outlines your approach and qualifications

• tries to persuade the client to accept your proposal.

Proposal content
The complexity of the proposal will depend on the size of the

project. Remember that the proposal needs the critical information included, but should not be over-cumbersome, unless you are dealing with a government bureaucracy.

- *Table of contents.* Only for long, complex proposals.

- *Background information.* Include a summary of the background information that you have gathered in the meetings. This will normally include details about the company, the current business environment, current challenges, and key people involved.

- *Purpose.* Give the purpose of the proposed engagement and objectives.

- *Objectives.* Give a description of the key outcomes that you expect from the consulting assignment. This may also include details on critical deliverables.

- *Approach.* Give a description of the critical steps and methodologies that will be used in the consulting assignment, the scope of the project and a plan.

- *Content.* Give the key areas in which service will be provided.

- *Pricing summary.* Give the compensation amount expected for the critical steps (see Chapter 7 for more information about rates). This will also include payment terms and cancellation fees.

- *Progress checks.* For longer-term projects, this will include information about interim progress reports, deliverables and critical milestones in the project.

- *Qualifications.* If this is the first time you have worked with the client you may need to include a summary of qualifications, client list and possible references.

- *Resources.* Again, if this is a large contract, include a definition of other consultants to be used.

- *Responsibilities.* List your responsibilities as well as the client's.

Proposal guidelines
- Be sure not to give away too much information in your proposal. Give only enough to make the prospective client want to come back and ask for more. If you provide too much advice and/or data, the client may decide to do the work him or herself.

- It is not generally a good idea to send a generic proposal. You need to meet and spend time with the prospective client in order to understand as much as possible what his or her needs are, then the proposal can be specifically tuned to those needs. (Since it is sometimes impossible actually to meet, this step may be done on the telephone, but a face-to-face meeting is always preferable.)

- A proposal should not take more than two to four hours to prepare. One to two is optimal.

- When facing competition for a project, remember that someone always has the inside track. Consultants refer to this as being 'wired'. The first question you need to ask yourself, then, is whether you have the inside track. Is there someone within the organisation who will push for you and keep you in the running? Try to keep these key people on your side.

    Competitors also have sponsors who are usually different from yours. You can estimate your chances of getting the assignment by comparing the power of your sponsor with the power of competitors' sponsors. Under certain circumstances you will not have the inside track but you should bid anyway because this may provide a chance for person-to-person exposure to the client. More importantly, the client may also have future projects, and if impressed with you, he or she may engage you for them.

Presenting the proposal

Always ask to present your proposal in person. This serves two purposes:

- It indicates how serious you are about the client and his or her project.

- A presentation in person increases your chances of clinching the sale.

After presenting the proposal, you will want some indication that the client has selected you as a consultant. You must take the initiative to finalise the sale. You close the sale by simply asking or by estimating when you are going to start. Once the client chooses you as a consultant, send a letter of understanding to confirm your arrangement.

USING COVER LETTERS

If you do not personally present your proposal, or if you are unable to contact the prospective client by phone, it is often a good idea to send a cover letter with the proposal or with the information about your services. Cover letters are used to:

- build rapport with the client
- introduce your objective for contacting them
- reaffirm information you know about them
- outline your qualifications
- ask for a close.

A cover letter should include the following information:

- *Reason for writing.* Article, referral, advertisement, research, previous meeting.
- *Summary of services.* Brief overview of range of services and experience.
- *Summary of perceived need.* The need the client may have based on your previous information, and how you could help them meet that need.
- *Close.* Ask for the next step, whether it is an appointment, a phone conversation or a confirmation.

FORMALISING CONTRACTS

Consultants, like everyone else, are turning to written contracts to protect their interests. Contracts do have a useful purpose other than self-protection. The consultant–client relationship is ambiguous and a clear contract provides a guide for both parties. A legal contract is an agreement enforceable by law. Contracts can be written, spoken or implied. You may wish to send a letter outlining the responsibilities of each party in the contract. An oral agreement is just as binding but more difficult to prove.

When creating a contract you should consider including the following items:

- Responsibilities of each party.

- Time agreements.

- Financial arrangements.

- Products or services to be delivered.

- Co-operation of client.

- Independent contractor's status. This establishes that you are not an employee.

- Advisory capacity. This indicates that you will not make decisions for the client, but will provide best opinions only.

- Client responsibility for review, implementation and result.

- Your potential work with competitors.

- Authority of client to contract for your services.

- Solicitor's fee clause.

- Limitations.

Using a legal contract is a personal decision. The majority of consultants do not use them. However, if you have had problems with clients, or this is the first time you are working with a client, or you are taking a substantial risk, then a contract is appropriate. Proper groundwork, continual communication and a thorough proposal may be an adequate substitute for a contract.

Now that you have learned how to sell your services, you need to decide how you will finance your business. But first take a few moments to review the checklist, case studies, and action points below.

CHECKLIST

Have you:

1. Written down the benefits to you of selling?

2. Highlighted in your database your 40–50 suspects?

3. Picked out any interesting prospects?

4. Created your introductory purpose and script?

5. Decided who will be the first 20 people you will contact?

6. Identified the outcome you require from these 20 calls?

7. Fixed three meetings with influencers, decision-makers and prospects?

8. Created a list of questions to ask prospects?

9. Practised paraphrasing and probing for specifics?

10. Created a template for proposals?

CASE STUDIES

Marie is an enthusiastic salesperson

Marie created her purpose and story and tried it out by calling friends and leaving messages with them to obtain feedback on her voice, tone, etc. She believes, because the type of training she does is short-term, she will need at least five active clients at any one time. Since then, she has made her first 40 telephone calls, by allocating two mornings a week for her telephone marketing efforts. She is using her time management system to track who she calls and the responses she is obtaining. She managed to speak to five people directly from those calls. She left a comprehensive message with others, based on the outline in the chapter.

Of those five people she managed to talk to directly, every call had a positive outcome. She received four more names of people who might be interested in her services, and she scheduled two meetings. One meeting was with a training broker, who might be able to sub-contract work to her. The other was with a retail company that might require some team building programmes. This lead came from someone she used to work for at another company who had just taken over as Director of Human Resources. Even with the messages she left, she received calls back from over 40 per cent of the individuals she had called. She sent the two people who gave her names thank you letters.

In her meeting with the retail company she was able to gather lots of information about the extent of the training the company had undertaken and identified that there probably would be much more work beyond the sales training. She needs to create a proposal, which she then needs to deliver personally to the Director of Human Resources, Vice President of Stores and a Regional Manager next week. She asked in the meeting if they were considering any other competitive bids, but they are not, so she believes she is well on the way to obtaining her first contract!

Frank is using his contacts to build his business

Frank has established and prioritised his database, and has focused on sending e-mail flyers to his key contacts. He found the target of 40 calls frightening, so he settled for ten key decision-makers instead. He believes that for his sort of services, long-term contract work, he needs only 2–3 prospects and ten suspects, because each assignment could last several months. He sent each of these people an e-mail note outlining what he was planning to do, and then followed up a week later with the phone calls. In addition he has made direct calls to several people with whom he used to work.

He was able to talk to five people, after two or three callbacks, which resulted in a meeting with a server company. The meeting was with the current vice president who used to be his boss at a previous organisation. The meeting is planned for next week, and while the VP seems to want only a short-term needs assessment project, Frank feels fairly confident he will be able to take this short-term project and build more work from it.

In addition, he has scheduled two meetings with other consultants in the industry, to start to build a collaborative network and to find out more about how they market and sell their services.

Linda waits for sales

Linda has been unable to create a network of 200 people, because she feels uncomfortable asking for help, and she doesn't think she knows that many people. Linda has dispatched a brochure and letter to several people. Some of the brochures have gone to those she knows, but she also decided to buy a small mailing list from the trade association of which she is a member. She has written on the cover letter for people to call her back, and she feels uncomfortable soliciting business. She feels that if there is an interest, people will call her. She has made one phone call to the five people who had said they might have work for her, but she feels she is being too pushy if she follows up with another call in under a week. So far, none of those five people has called her back.

She has met several people for lunch, but they have been more like general networking and socialising meetings rather than business development opportunities. She is finding that time is hanging on her hands, and is concerned that her severance package will not last long enough to carry her over until the first business comes in.

ACTION POINTS

1. In terms of the sales process, what tools and techniques will you use to ensure that you are conducting activities in all of the critical stages in business development: network, suspects, prospects, proposals and clients? How long do you believe the sales process is for your type of business? How many people do you think you need in each category to be successful?

2. How many telephone calls do you think would be appropriate for your type of business? How will you ensure that you are practising the key skills when making telephone calls? What is the target you will set yourself and how will you measure your success?

3. What meetings will you schedule? How will you ensure that you are using these meetings to gather information and not just talk? How can you practise asking open-ended questions and listening? What type of proposal is required for your business? How much legal protection is required for your business?

7

Financing Your Business

Funding a consulting business, establishing fee rates and collecting outstanding accounts receivable is often one of the most misunderstood and underestimated areas of a consulting business. In this chapter, we will guide you through the process of estimating the funds you need, and then show you how to ensure you charge enough to make your consulting business profitable.

ESTIMATING YOUR START-UP COSTS

Every business faces one-time start-up costs, which are dependent on the type of consulting you are doing, your location and your plans.

You must systematically plan also for all monthly expenses. The following is a checklist of possible areas of cost:

- rent
- office preparation
- computer and printer
- telephone
- fax
- other office equipment and furniture
- utilities
- postage
- stationery and business cards
- insurance
- printing and supplies
- answering service
- typing services
- accounting and legal services
- business licences and permits
- advertising and promotion
- dues and subscriptions
- books and reference materials
- travel
- conventions

- continuing education
- entertainment
- gifts
- salaries
- unemployment insurance
- miscellaneous.

As you are starting your business, the two areas of cost that tend to be immediately higher than the others are your phone bill and eating-out expenses. When you first begin marketing your business, as we discussed in Chapters 5 and 6, the telephone becomes a time-effective business development tool. You might expect, depending on your speed and proficiency on the phone, your phone bill to at least double in the early months. In addition, much of the time you spend with networking contacts will be over food of some kind – breakfast, coffee, lunch, dinner, etc! It is important to try to minimise eating out – meetings can be held separately from meals. And, while it may be tempting to pick up the bill as this is now a deductible business expense, as a worthwhile accountant would say, 'Don't spend money to save money!'

You need to have a certain amount of money in reserve on which to live while your business gets started. You need a minimum of six months' living money, but the optimum is one year's. Keep in mind that most companies pay invoices a certain number of weeks after they are received. On average, payment time is six weeks. In addition, it may take you some time to close your first contract, and then you have to work for a period of time before you can invoice some work. You must factor this in when creating your cash flow.

You also need to have some money in reserve in case you get sick and can't work for any amount of time, or if someone close to you becomes ill and you need to care for them, etc. Another good reason to have some cash reserves is so that you do not appear desperate when selling. You will sell more effectively if you're not too hungry. If you are too eager, the customer may pick up on it and wonder if you're good enough. Let's look at how you can fund your business in this start-up phase.

FINDING SOURCES OF CAPITAL

Once you have calculated your profit and loss and cash flow statement, and estimated your start-up costs, you should be able to calculate how much income you need in order to source your business. There are various options for funding your business.

- **Bank loan**. When dealing with a bank you should provide the business plan, look the part, and be prepared to shop around for a bank to back you.

- **Friends/venture capital**. More often than you might suspect, you can find friends who believe in your undertaking more than your banker does. There are also a range of venture capital firms that will often finance new businesses. People with venture capital often want a greater portion of the company ownership. In addition, there are some entrepreneurs who will fund start-ups. One consultant obtained private funding from the CEO of the company that was employing her.

- **Savings**. More often than not, your own personal savings are adequate to finance your start-up as a consultant. You will need approximately a year's worth of income as a back-up resource.

- **Selling shares**. You may consider selling some shares of stock to finance your start.

- **Redundancy packages**. You may use funds received from your previous company when laid off.

- **Credit cards**. Many people with service businesses have financed themselves with credit cards since this has been the only credit available to them. Bear in mind that this is the most expensive way to finance since most credit card companies charge very high interest rates. However, many credit cards offer low introductory rates and will help consolidate your previous debt. For example, the founder of a consulting firm who was 36, had three children under 12, and was the main breadwinner, funded his start-up business with credit cards. The business ultimately grossed £20 million, with 25 per cent net profit. He definitely covered his credit card interest!

- **Equity line of credit**. Many banks and financial institutions will offer equity lines of credit on a primary property which can be used to fund business growth. The equity line of credit needs to be established while you are still employed.

- **The moonlighting plan**. Keep your full-time job and develop your business as a sideline. When it takes off you can go full-time. But be sure to work at least eight hours a week on the sideline business.

- **The part-time plan**. Work a part-time job to provide a base income while you are building up the business. When your business equals the base income, drop the part-time job.

- **The spin-off plan**. Turn your previous employer into your first major customer, or, when ethically possible, take a major client with you from your previous job. Often organisations will place limitations on the extent to which this is possible. For example, IBM will not take back previous employees as sub-contractors within the first year. Many organisations therefore have arisen who act as a broker between the client and the prior employee to avoid this limitation.

- **The piggyback plan**. If you have a working spouse or partner, cut back on your expenses and live on one salary until the business gets going.

- **Borrowing from retirement funds**. It is often possible to borrow against retirement funds.

ESTABLISHING FINANCIAL OBJECTIVES

You need to establish financial objectives for your business within the finance Key Result Area. Again, these objectives need to meet the **SMART** criteria:

S – Specific
M – Measurable
A – Aligned
R – Results-oriented
T – Time-based.

There is normally a variety of financial objectives for a consulting business under several categories:

- sales revenue
- profit
- gross margin
- fee structure
- ageing percentage
- cash flow.

Setting clear objectives for the financial side of your business will help to ensure you make your business successful and viable.

CREATING REVENUE AND CASH FLOW STATEMENTS

In managing business performance, there are two critical financial reports: the revenue statement and the cash flow statement. Let's look at the details in the revenue statement first. The revenue statement shows monthly invoice amounts and costs.

Revenue statement

When you are getting started, based on your business plan, calculate your estimated revenue for the first year that will include all income from your business. If your business is already operating, the revenue figure will comprise the total of your invoices. For example, if you wish to invoice £600 a day, and you budget on working ten days a month, your revenue figure will be £6,000 each month. In addition, you may have other income from materials and sales of products. Each will be budgeted in the month the sale takes place, not necessarily when the income comes in. (See Figure 23.)

Month	Jan	Feb	Mar	Apr	May	June	July	Aug	Sept	Oct	Nov	Dec
Consulting income	6,000	6,000	6,000	6,000	6,000	6,000	6,000	6,000	6,000	6,000	6,000	6,000
Materials	500	500	500	500	500	500	500	500	500	500	500	500
Revenue	6,500	6,500	6,500	6,500	6,500	6,500	6,500	6,500	6,500	6,500	6,500	6,500

Fig. 23. Revenue statement.

Costs

Your costs will include sales, marketing, salaries, rent, equipment, utilities and so on as listed at the beginning of this chapter. (See Figure 24.) These costs include:

- **fixed costs,** which are costs which occur whether or not there are sales: utilities, cost of your car, etc.

- **variable costs**, which are those you would not have incurred if you had not made a sale: printing of materials, sub-contractors' expenses, etc.

Month	Jan	Feb	Mar	Apr	May	June	July	Aug	Sept	Oct	Nov	Dec
Car	250	250	250	250	250	250	250	250	250	250	250	250
Rent	500	500	500	500	500	500	500	500	500	500	500	500
Materials	250	250	250	250	250	250	250	250	250	250	250	250
Phone	250	250	250	250	250	250	250	250	250	250	250	250
Cost	1,250	1,250	1,250	1,250	1,250	1,250	1,250	1,250	1,250	1,250	1,250	1,250

Fig. 24. Cost statement.

Profit/loss

After you have added up all your costs and subtracted them from your invoiced sales revenue, you have your profit/loss. Profits are usually stated as a percentage of your total sales revenue (see Figure 25). From the difference between revenue and costs, you will need to pay both yourself and taxes. What is left is your net profit.

Month	Jan	Feb	Mar	Apr	May	June	July	Aug	Sept	Oct	Nov	Dec
Revenue	6,500	6,500	6,500	6,500	6,500	6,500	6,500	6,500	6,500	6,500	6,500	6,500
Cost	1,250	1,250	1,250	1,250	1,250	1,250	1,250	1,250	1,250	1,250	1,250	1,250
Gross margin	5,250	5,250	5,250	5,250	5,250	5,250	5,250	5,250	5,250	5,250	5,250	5,250
Percentage	80%	80%	80%	80%	80%	80%	80%	80%	80%	80%	80%	80%

Fig. 25. Profit/loss statement.

Many small companies now use computer-based software to help them manage the financial side of the business. QuickBooks^{TM} is currently the market leader in this area.

Cash flow statement

The cash flow analysis explains the amount and timing of expected cash flows both in and out. The cash flow statement is usually divided into the sources of the funds and the uses to which the funds are put. Sources of funds normally include sales revenue, owner investment, loans and outside equity investment. Use of funds is

Month	Jan	Feb	Mar	Apr	May	June	July	Aug	Sept	Oct	Nov	Dec
Cash				6,500	6,500	6,500	6,500	6,500	6,500	6,500	6,500	6,500
Cost	1,250	1,250	1,250	1,250	1,250	1,250	1,250	1,250	1,250	1,250	1,250	1,250
Profit	-1,250	-1,250	1,250	5,250	5,250	5,250	5,250	5,250	5,250	5,250	5,250	5,250
Percentage				80%	80%	80%	80%	80%	80%	80%	80%	80%

Fig. 26. Cash flow statement.

typically expenditures for rent, salaries, equipment, taxes, interest on loans and other costs. The purpose of the cash flow analysis is to determine whether you will have enough incoming sources of funds to meet required out-going uses. Continuing the previous examples, if all else remains constant, yet we use cash flow statements to manage the financial side of the business, you can see the difference in Figure 26.

In this example, we are assuming that the consulting work performed in January is invoiced at the end of January, but that payment does not take place until 60 days later, at the end of March. You will have to pay January, February and March costs before you receive any revenue. As you can see, with steady income and a 60-day payment term, it is critical to ensure an adequate cash flow. More businesses fail due to lack of cash then lack of clients so most consultants use the cash-in/cash-out approach to managing their business.

For example, one consultant had too much work for her to manage, and when she reviewed her workload, she decided that she could afford to pay a sub-contractor full-time for three months. However, when she began the work she discovered that she had to pay her sub-contractor immediately, but that she would not receive the income until three months later, and as a result had to use money from her savings to absorb the cost.

SETTING YOUR BILLING RATE

When people who are not consultants hear a billing rate, they often see the figure as astronomically high because they compare it with the salary they are earning, as if it was paid on an hourly basis. Unfortunately, this is not a fair comparison as the consultant's rate includes many factors that are included above and beyond the employee's salary.

Considerations

The consulting fees charged are your revenue and it is important when setting a billing rate to take into consideration the following nine items:

1. *Salary*. This is your worth as a labour commodity on the open market performing the same services you provide as a consultant.

2. *Research and development*. This is an important overhead expense in time and money, which is often forgotten. When you are employed, this is part of your overall compensation 'package'. This includes purchasing books, finding answers to questions, taking classes, purchasing new software, etc. As you continue to improve your skills or streamline your operations, this cost needs to be covered in your consulting fee.

3. *Employee benefits*. Benefits are the extras you receive from an employer, above and beyond your salary, which are often tax-free. For most employees, benefits amount to 25–60 per cent of their salary and include such items as insurance, training, holidays, sick leave, pension, unemployment insurance and payroll taxes. In addition, employers often match employees' contributions to retirement plans, medical coverage, etc. The consulting rate must cover all benefit costs.

4. *Overhead expenses*. Overheads represent the expenses incurred in operating a business and include both direct and indirect costs as described earlier. Expenses can include, but are not limited to, typing, telephone, car, travel, postage and delivery, lights, electricity, insurance, duplicating, and securing projects, e.g. proposal writing. When you work for another company, it is easy to forget that paper and pencils cost money that you must now spend yourself.

5. *Profit*. Profit is your reward for business risks and ownership, and ranges from 10–30 per cent of your gross revenue. Most business owners confuse revenue with profit.

6. *Competition*. When establishing your billing rate you must be aware of the customs of your community and of the industry. Three factors determine your competitive position:

(a) What are your successful competitors charging?

(b) What will your clients pay?

(c) What minimum and maximum levels will you accept?

If your rate is perceived as too low, prospective customers will assume you are not very good. If your rate is perceived as too high, you may put off prospective customers 'No wonder he can afford to drive a Mercedes!' Many trade associations will publish current rates, and it is always worth talking to others in the industry to evaluate current market levels.

7. *Economic conditions.* Your billing rate must take into account the economic conditions that affect you. Is there inflation, or a recession? At what rate are your costs rising or falling? When the market is doing well, this often produces a growth in the number of consultants required. However, conversely, a poor economic market may not indicate the opposite. Often, when the market is going down and companies are reducing their workforce, it creates more work for consultants to meet short-term needs.

8. *Bad debts.* A bad debt occurs when you are not paid for services you provide. Professional firms experience bad debt rates ranging from 5 to 40 per cent. Most try to maintain a 5–10 per cent bad-debt ratio. Ideas on how to ensure you collect the money owed to you are given later in this chapter.

9. *Fairness to clients.* After considering all the above items, you must then make an ethical judgement on what you think is fair to your clients and to yourself. One key issue is consistency in pricing. Within certain market segments, e.g. high-tech, it is important to have a consistent fee structure. For different market segments, you may have a different pricing structure, e.g. charge less to non-profit organisations than to high-tech companies. You may also have reasons for taking on a project that you know will cost you more than the company has budgeted. If this is the case, you still need to do your best work and not put in fewer hours because you are getting less than your regular rate.

Calculating your billing rate

This section will show you how to calculate your base hourly billing rate. Often you will not be charging clients on an hourly basis, but a fixed fee instead. Even so, this step is important to provide the starting point in calculating other approaches. Before the billing rate can be calculated, there are two important items that need to be defined:

1. *Billable hours.* These are the number of working hours you **actually bill** to clients. You may work more hours for the client but you may not charge for all of them.

The number of working hours in a year is estimated, simplistically, by taking the number of working weeks in a year as 48 and multiplying these by the approximate number of working hours in a week (41.66). The total of billable hours in a year is therefore 2,000.

2. *Your utilisation rate.* This tells you what percentage of total working hours each week/year you bill to clients. Try to bill 50–60 per cent of your available hours to a variety of clients. The rest of your time (40–50 per cent) is spent looking for work administering your business, training, taking holidays, etc. If you bill consistently more than 60 per cent, other parts of your business will suffer, often the marketing side, resulting in the feast or famine syndrome.

For example, based on a total number of billable hours of 2,000, and a 60 per cent utilisation rate, you will only be able to bill 1,200 hours.

Setting your base rate

This rule uses your salary requirements as a beginning to calculate your base-billing rate. In addition it assumes that every consultant generates overheads and benefits and that he or she should also produce a profit. Therefore multiply your salary requirement by two to arrive at total yearly target revenues. Then your hourly billing rate becomes your total yearly revenues divided by your yearly billable hours. This is a simple and quick method to calculate your base-billing rate. You only need to know your annual salary requirements and the number of hours you can bill to clients each year.

For example:

- If you require £40,000 a year salary, you need to generate twice that to ensure you have enough for profit, overheads and benefits = £80,000.

- If you wish to work at 60 per cent utilisation rate (1,200 hours per year), the base-billing rate would be £80,000, divided by 1,200.

- This equals a base rate of £66.66 per hour or approximately £550 per day.

In most industries there is an 'accepted' hourly rate, so the extent to which you can obtain the rate you wish depends on these industry standards. For example, technical writing has a market place rate of £40 per hour, software programming can range from £60 to £80 per hour, and training consultants range from £1,000 to £1,500 per day.

This calculation is valuable because if you cannot achieve a minimum hourly rate of £40 per hour, you will be forced to work too many hours, which may result in missing critical aspects of managing your business.

USING DIFFERENT FEE ARRANGEMENTS

There are certain common fee arrangements. Many consultants use different fee arrangements depending on the nature of the project.

Hourly or time charges

Hourly or time charges involve multiplying your billing rate by the number of hours you work for the client. This is the most basic and the most common fee arrangement. All you need is your standard billing rate and a method to keep track of how you spend your time.

The benefit to you is that you are paid for all the hours you work and there is minimum risk to you. The disadvantage to the client with this structure is that they do not know how much the project will cost, and they have less control of the cost outcome. It can feel like a 'bottomless pit' to them. For example, a client used a consultant on an hourly rate to develop three procedure manuals. All the money allocated to it was gone by the time the first manual was completed.

Fixed fees

Fixed fees occur when a particular service is performed for a fixed amount. The disadvantage is that you as the consultant run the risk of budget overruns, but you gain the bonus of budget underruns. Generally, if you quote a certain fee and it requires more time than expected, you absorb the difference. A clear project definition and statement of milestones and deliverables are key.

The rule of thumb for deciding how much to charge for a fixed fee contract is to take the numbers of hours you think the work will take, and multiply by two (minimum) or three (maximum). For example, a consultant was working on a fixed fee bid to upgrade an organisation's existing applications and install several new applications. Because he had an incomplete understanding of the system requirements when he started the job, the installation took over four times the hours he had budgeted. That type of project can kill the hourly rate!

So the advantage to you of this fee structure is that it can hide your daily rate. However, the disadvantage to you is that you are taking a risk and might not get paid for all the hours you work. The project can change, the client can try to add additional steps, change his or her mind, or not provide the information you require, etc. To lessen your risk, you must have a very clear outline with the specifics of the project. Then, if you are asked to do extra, you can happily agree, but since the terms of the contract have changed, you need to negotiate more money.

Often customers prefer this fee structure since they know ahead exactly how much the project will cost.

Bracket fees
Bracket fees combine fixed fees and time charges. Essentially you work on an hourly basis but your fee cannot exceed a specific amount. This fee structure favours the client and protects them from budget overruns.

Percentage fees
Merger and acquisition consultants may charge a percentage of the entire transaction known as a percentage fee.

Assignment fees
As a consultant, you may perform projects that have intrinsic value beyond the number of days or hours consumed. Assignment fees are additional payments for such projects and can be either fixed amounts or percentages.

Retainer fees
Retainer fees have several meanings among consultants. They may describe an advanced payment to retain your services for a particular project. In this respect it is a sign of faith on the client's part to use your services and to ensure payment.

In a slightly different sense, retainers are used to guarantee your availability during a certain time period. Clients use retainer fees to ensure continuity of services. Consultants like retainer fees because they provide a steady income. There are also some challenges associated with a retainer. Clients may confuse a retainer with a salary, and overload your time. Conversely the client may become absorbed in his or her internal responsibilities and not give you the work that you have budgeted. While this looks positive in the short term for the consultant (being paid for not working!) in the long term, this will cause the client to be dissatisfied and go elsewhere. In order to gain the most from this fee structure, make sure you specify in detail what is included and what isn't; for example, phone calls (how many), time at the client's site (number of hours), written communication required, etc. This type of payment is common for such consultants as psychologists, legal counsel, etc.

Equity fees

Occasionally consultants receive payment from clients in the form of business ownership in the client's company. This may be an option if the client does not want to pay your published rate. However, it is a high-risk option and you want to make sure you balance these types of high-risk compensation with firm payment.

Deferred fees

A deferred fee is not really a method of determining your fee. Instead it is a collection method that pays you in instalments over an extended time period. Deferred fees are used most often when the client does not have the money to pay you. The client may also request deferred fees so that the savings from the project can offset your consulting fee as it comes due. If you are accepting deferred fees, you are extending credit to your clients. To offset these risks, you should consider the following tactics employed by many professionals:

• Charge interest on the total amount.

• Charge higher fees.

• Request a sizeable retainer fee before you start the project.

• Request collateral if your total fees are substantial.

• Request payment via cashier's check or credit card to ensure payment.

Be sure the company is solvent before you reach any agreement about deferred fees.

Extras

If you charge travel time, learning time, meals, etc., this should be discussed and agreed upon up-front. Many organisations will not pay for travel or mileage if you are travelling within the same area as employees of the company do.

There should be no surprises on the invoice. In addition, if you have to travel a long distance, consider charging a lower daily rate for the travel day. While you are not able to work the entire day, you may be able to complete some preparation work on the journey, so the entire day is not lost.

While we have included details on all the different fee structures, you may want to concentrate on one or two options so that the pricing arrangement is not too complex.

Guidelines for asking for fees

The rate that consultants can charge for their services is usually influenced by their confidence in asking. If the client suspects from your body language that you are uncomfortable with the rate, he or she will try to negotiate to reduce it. If there is confidence in your approach the client is less likely to try and reduce the rate.

- Remember you can always reduce the rate: it is much harder to ask for more!

- Sometimes consultants are willing to ask for less money if the contract is in an area of interest where they receive the benefit of learning more.

- Often consultants on long-term assignments give a price break on their daily rate. Remember if you do this that you will still have to build up your business again after you have finished the assignment, and you will need the money from that daily rate to do so.

- When you work half a day, you need to assess whether you can actually use the other half-day. Often consultants charge 75–100 per cent for a half-day for this reason.

COLLECTING FEES

You can avoid many fee collection problems through good front-end communication. As early as possible, obtain a mutual understanding with your client concerning the fee. As a general practice, discuss your fees during the first meeting, and indicate how and when billing occurs. Many consultants find it difficult to discuss fees with prospective clients. Some fear losing the consulting project if their fees seem too high, some are reluctant to discuss money, and other consultants are so involved with discussing the project they forget to discuss the fees.

LIMITING YOUR EXPOSURE TO BAD DEBTS

Though you need to make an allowance for bad debts, there are certain things you can do to avoid not getting paid:

- Obtain progress payments by billing frequently. A business can budget £1,000 per month more easily than it can absorb a £12,000 bill at year's end.

- Bill on time: the value of your service diminishes in the client's mind over time.

- Establish a billing and collecting practice.

- Make sure you obtain purchase orders (POs) wherever possible.

- Don't work without a PO.

- Make sure you have a clear contract with defined payment terms.

- Once the contract is signed, ask up-front about the company's procedures for paying vendors. What do I need to do to get paid? What is your process? Who has to sign off on bills?

- Work in milestones throughout the duration of the contract.

- Ask if you can bill weekly/bi-weekly/monthly/bi-monthly.

- Communicate clearly your normal payment terms.

- Some consultants charge late fees. However, large organisations such as Sun and Oracle will not pay them.

- You may ask for a deposit up-front.

- Check out the financial status of the company beforehand. Read trade publications, ask other vendors, etc.

- Decide when to stop working if you are not getting paid. Many consultants have horror stories of being owed tens of thousands of pounds. Either set a time period for yourself or an amount beyond which you will withhold services (such as over 90 days or £10,000). It is surprising how quickly a cheque can be written when you say you will stop working.

Your greatest friends in a company are those in the accounts department. Do not alienate them, but engage their help to solve your problems if you are not getting paid on time.

CHARGING FOR SUB-CONTRACTING

Sub-contracting works both ways. You can sub-contract work to other consultants when you need help. This means you are the main contractor and the other consultants are your sub-contractors. In addition, you can do work for another consultant, who has the main client contact. This means that you are the sub-contractor.
. While this process is very beneficial to both parties, it can also lead to misunderstandings if the working parameters are not clear up-front.

Sub-contracting work to others

When you have too much work, a viable option is to sub-contract the work to other consultants. Bear in mind the following guidelines:

- Make sure you have worked with the consultants previously so that you know their competencies and their liabilities.

- Keep in mind that when you hire sub-contractors you are responsible for them and the work they produce.

- Be clear about the work they will be doing, the standards that you expect and the measurements that will be put in place.

- Be clear about the financial remuneration, not only the amount to be paid, but also the payment terms that you will adhere to.

- Make sure the sub-contractor realises that all invoicing will be done through you.

- Make sure the sub-contractor realises that this is your client. Any further work from the client, even if the sub-contractor sells it him or herself, must come through you.

Who owns the client?

This is often the biggest bone of contention when working with sub-contractors. Most consultants do not realise the complexity of getting the first 'foot in the door' and then want to own the remainder of the work. Some consultants use contracts to try to enforce this structure, but it is better to have a clear mutual understanding when you begin the assignment.

For example, one consultant sub-contracted a technical writing project through a business brokerage. The sub-contractor had to sign a contract stating that she could not work for that client directly for the next year. For this organisation, there was only one purchaser of technical writing. It was appropriate in this case that the sub-contractor was unable to do business directly with the organisation.

Another consultant began work for a large organisation conducting training programmes. A brokerage firm that he sub-contracted for also did work in that organisation, but with several different contacts. The brokerage tried to prevent the consultant from working with that organisation. This was inappropriate because the consultant had several direct contacts, and there were multiple points of entry into the company.

The main way to decide whether a client belongs to you or the other consultant normally comes from the point of entry into the organisation: who had the first contact?

Doing sub-contract work for others
This can be a good way to get work when you have time available and also when you are still developing your qualifications. Sub-contracting is like the cake without icing. It enables you to obtain exposure, put clients on your reference list and gain some stable income. However, it is not as financially lucrative as working with clients directly. Here are two guidelines about working as a sub-contractor:

- Be clear about the work you will be doing, the standards the contractor expects and the measurements that will be put in place.

- Be clear about the financial remuneration, not only the amount to be paid, but also the payment terms that you will accept.

Financial compensation for sub-contracting
The general industry standard allows the consultant or consulting organisation that gets the work to keep approximately 50 per cent of the revenue. The ability to market the service and collect the revenue is worth half of the total. Remember, most consultants can do the work, but many cannot find it.

Now that you have decided how to finance your business and how much to charge for your services, in Chapter 8 we will look at how to get organised. But first, take a few minutes to review the checklist, case studies and action points.

CHECKLIST

Have you:

1. Established financial objectives for your business?
2. Created a cash flow statement?
3. Estimated your start-up costs?
4. Decided how you will fund yourself for six months to a year?
5. Calculated your base-billing rate?
6. Decided whether you wish to price your service by project?
7. Decided how to limit your exposure to bad debts?
8. Researched sub-contracting options as a base source of income?

CASE STUDIES

Marie charges per project/per person

Marie set a financial objective for her business: she wants to generate the same amount in revenue as the salary she received when she was employed. She knows this is not as much money, but she thinks it is realistic for the first year. She has extended the equity line of credit on her house, and has six months in savings. She already has a computer at home, and she knows her main start-up cost will be eating out and phone calls. She has decided to try to have meetings separately from meals, but is prepared for the rise in phone calls, since she knows this is a critical start-up cost for her.

She has calculated her base-billing rate at £1,000 per day for large training and development projects. She will use this rate for quoting the sales training project, as this will be a large, customised programme. She believes this will cover some development and marketing time. From this base assumption, for her other standard training programmes she is going to charge per person per day, since this is a common practice in the industry. She will charge a graduated scale based on numbers of people ranging from £100 to £150 per person per day. She has contacted a training broker for whom she wishes to sub-contract work. Although the training broker has over 40 large, high-tech clients, she believes the exposure to these clients as she is getting started will prove to be extremely beneficial. She accepts that she will be paid only £400 per day for this work, but feels that the corresponding benefits outweigh the revenue shortfall.

Frank charges a fixed daily rate

Frank has sold some of his shares in one of his previous organisations to provide his back-up capital. He has built a clear cash flow statement based on the assumption that he will receive his first client within three months, and they will pay their first invoice three months later. He wants to charge a 50 per cent deposit up-front then collect payment on the rest of the work, but he realises that, as this is his first contract, he will probably have to hold off on invoicing up-front this time. He realises that most of his assignments will be long term with a fixed number of days, so he has calculated a daily rate of £650 per day, for contracts over 20 days. His first contract with the Server Company is for 20 days over a three-month period, with each stage comprising ten days' work. Each stage has concrete, measurable steps and deliverables.

Each stage will be invoiced separately: the first after five days' and ten days' work, the second at the beginning and end of the work. He has talked to the accounts department and understands their payment process. He knows he has to have a signed PO from the director, issue an invoice to both the director and accounts who then asks the director to approve the signature. The invoice will be paid at 45 days. He believes his knowledge of this system will prevent any exposure to bad debts.

Linda charges an hourly rate

Linda is using her six-month severance package to live, and is investing in equipment. She decided to establish her rate at £750 per day, but then a friend called and asked if she wanted to work full-time for three months as a contract financial manager while the existing manager was on maternity leave. The pay was only £30 per hour, but Linda accepted since she was demoralised at the lack of work. She still believed this job would end up being lucrative for her since it was twice as much as she was earning when she was full-time. What she forgot was that she had no benefits or paid holiday included in this money. In addition, she had no time to market during this three-month period and none of the people she has called has called her back.

ACTION POINTS

1. As you set the financial objectives for your business, what is a realistic target revenue figure and how will you protect your cash flow as you are getting started? Think about what other financial safeguards you could put in place to fund your start-up.

2. As you looked at the industry, what do you believe is the market rate for the type of services you offer? Are your contract opportunities short term or long term, and how will this affect the pricing structure? What is the base minimum compensation you will accept? What types of fee structures would be appropriate for your business?

3. To what extent is acting as a sub-contractor to others a viable option for you? Who do you know in your industry who might have opportunities to provide you with work? If you sub-contract to others what will be the lowest rate you will accept? Who do you know in your network that you think you could use if you had too much work? What contractual arrangement will you have with these sub-contractors?

8

Organising Your Business

Unlike when you work for an organisation, there is no automatic structuring system when you are running your own consulting business. The ability to organise activities and structure your environment is critical to being successful as a consultant. In this chapter, we will review the principles behind getting organised when you get started, including setting up your office, plus give you ideas and tips for ongoing office organisation and activity planning.

SETTING UP YOUR ORGANISATION STRUCTURE

Creating your office space

There are two options open to consultants:

- work from home
- set up a separate office.

Below we have listed some advantages and disadvantages of both options.

Working from home: advantages
- Saves costs.

- Avoids commuting: the two-second commute!

- Most work can be performed from home.

- Fewer 'work' clothes. (You can look like Edward Scissorhands when talking to clients and they won't know!)

- Flexibility in that you can work your own hours.

Working from home: disadvantages
- Interruptions from family.

- No place to receive visitors.

- Lack of professional image.

- People think you're not really working.

- Separate phone lines are essential.

- Difficulty in distancing yourself from the business.

- Office space can be a 'red flag' to the taxman if you claim deductions for a home office.

- There can be complications when you sell your house, because you are now selling a house and an office.

Working from an office: advantages
- Distance from home.

- Prestige.

- Proximity to clients.

- Referral potential.

Working from an office: disadvantages
- Cost.

- Distance from home.

- Less convenient when you want to refer to paperwork.

Possible solutions
- Rent a small office.

- Share an office with other professionals. You may even be able to barter services for space.

- Use an executive suite.

- Sublet an office.

The key factor to remember when making the decision on office space is to ensure you have a dedicated space and you can separate/ close off the office area from your home. Trying to share a child's bedroom is not conducive to productive work. Often when consultants are beginning their consulting practice, working at home is the simplest, most expedient option, and to this end it is worth working out ways to overcome the disadvantages.

Furniture
Consultants require minimal office furniture:

- desk
- chair
- filing cabinets
- bookshelf.

Equipment, software and support tools

Telephone
It is essential to have both a dedicated telephone line and a line dedicated to the fax and e-mail when working from home. Often consultants use three dedicated lines: one for the phone, one for the fax, and one for e-mail. Sharing a home line can cause inconvenience to other family members and might appear unprofessional. ISDN is also an option. In addition, a cell phone can be an essential tool if you are on the move a lot.

E-mail
As the World-Wide Web expands, some type of e-mail system is critical. It can be used for researching companies and for marketing and maintaining contact with individuals when you are busy. The e-mail provider does not need to be the same as the web site provider.

Answering service
You must decide on some type of answering service for your telephone to ensure you do not miss important business calls. The following are some of the options available to you.

- Answering machine with remote dial-in capabilities: while this is cheaper, the quality of the voice message is often not high.

- Answering service: high cost and hard to guarantee the quality.

- Voicemail: this provides the highest quality reception and most flexibility in terms of remote checking, and saving of messages.

Personal computer
It is essential for a consultant to own a personal computer. The choice between an IBM (or IBM clone) or a Macintosh depends on the nature of the work you perform, your degree of computer literacy, and the equipment your prospective clients use.

Printer
A laser printer is an ideal investment depending on the number of

written documents you need to produce. Many printers available now have colour printing options, and can also serve as a copier. Your choice of printer is related to the type of business that you operate.

Wordprocessing software
The most popular versions on the market are WordPerfect™ and Microsoft Word™.

Spreadsheet
Lotus 1-2-3™ and Excel™ are the most widely used.

Database
ACT™ is an excellent sales tracking system. You can also use a more basic labels program. The purpose is to ensure you have a computer record of all prospects and clients.

Graphics program
The program you choose again depends on the nature of the graphics you need to produce. Popular packages are Harvard Graphics™, Page Maker™ and Power Point™.

Cash management
Software such as QuickBooks™ is excellent for tracking finances, including revenue and costs.

Fax machine
Having access to a fax machine is essential in today's business market. Options include either a stand-alone machine or a computer-based version. The advantage of a stand-alone is that it works whether the computer is on-line or not. The disadvantage is that material is received, but not in soft copy format.

A computer-based version can be slightly more inconvenient to use, but the advantage is that documents can be sent directly from the computer. The disadvantage is that if the computer is not powered up, documents cannot be sent or received.

As with other business decisions, it is important to analyse the business requirements and then decide the best tool for the needs.

Stationery
Stationery is the primary means of establishing a professional image and identity. It is often a good idea to keep it flexible to allow you to

change the content as the business develops. Types of stationery and guidelines for using are detailed below:

Business cards
- Quality paper stock.

- Conservative (based on profession).

- Include name, company name, telephone number, fax number, e-mail address and type of consulting.

Letterhead
Same quality paper stock and layout as business card.

Second sheet
Same quality paper stock as letterhead.

Envelopes
Same quality paper stock and layout as the letterhead. You can also use labels that can be used on any type of envelope.

Many consultants focus on the design and the layout of their stationery and forget that people buy people, not paper. More importantly, many written communications are now sent by fax and e-mail, and therefore the quality of the stationery becomes less important.

Clothes and image
Your clothes and accessories need to match the image you wish to portray based on your area of consulting and your prospective client base. Your clothes and image need to reflect who you are and what clients expect from you. A marketing consultant in the Midlands dressed in such clothes as a purple jacket and yellow trousers – no one doubted he was in the design business!

Administrative support
Often we cannot cope with all our administrative requirements ourselves. This is an area that we include in our business plan when we are considering resources. Options include:

Do it yourself
This is OK if you are computer literate, but it also depends on the kind of work you do.

Temporary agency
Most areas offer administrative support services. Try to ensure the software used by the agency is compatible with your software so that business information is interchangeable.

Executive suite
Often the services of a typist are available at extra cost at an executive suite.

Contractual administrative support
Many consultants will invoice clients for the administrative support they need, at the cost they pay, or with a minimal mark-up. This ensures a win-win solution. The client pays a lower rate than if the consultant does the work. The consultant does not take on any additional expenses.

Company-provided administrative support
Many organisations will supply internal editing and administrative support with projects if this reduces the overall cost of the assignment.

Employed staff
This is expensive and there will probably not be enough work, at least at the beginning, to justify an employee's salary. In the early stages of your practice, you probably will have no need for employed staff. The general rule applies that you only need personnel if you are billing over 80 per cent of your time, or if you can bill over 70 per cent of that person's time.

Sub-contractors
It is a good idea to establish a network of possible sub-contractors, which enables you to take larger contracts, exposes you to other sources of revenue and can position you more favourably in comparison with the other larger consulting firms.

ORGANISING YOUR PAPER FLOW

Organising your office and paper flow is important to ensuring your productivity. Often filing systems tend to develop in demand to paper, when they should help manage paperwork to achieve objectives. A category-focused filing system consists of four main sections:

1. Current files relating to achieving short-term milestones.

2 Bring-forward files to track future actions related to objectives.

3. Current hanging files for paperwork related to current objectives, within Key Result Areas.

4. Historical files for objectives, within Key Result Areas.

Current files: paper for today
These can be sorted by objective, customer, etc., and are usually stored on the desk, in stacking trays or folders.

Bring-forward files
Bring-forward files (sometimes called tickler files) can be located in hanging files or on the computer. Bring-forward files consist of numbered folders, one for each day of the month (31), and one for each month of the next six months (6).

Requests for action are placed in the folder under the day the action must start.

At the end of each day, you must check the folder to see what's coming up for the next day. Once each week look at the folder for the coming month and move forward any items which need to be in the 31-day files.

Current project files: per Key Result Area
It is important to distinguish between current information, which needs to be readily available for possible action, and historical information, which is complete.

Current project files are normally located in your desk drawer and contain all current paperwork, divided by Key Result Area, if at all possible. The files can be colour coded to indicate different activities, e.g. prospecting could be red, existing clients green.

Historical data files: per Key Result Area
These files contain information which is complete and may be needed for future reference. There is a legal obligation to keep certain types of paperwork. The risk with historical files is that far too much information is kept, most of which is unlikely to be needed in the future. Historical files are also categorised by Key Result Area and need to be cleared out at least once every three months.

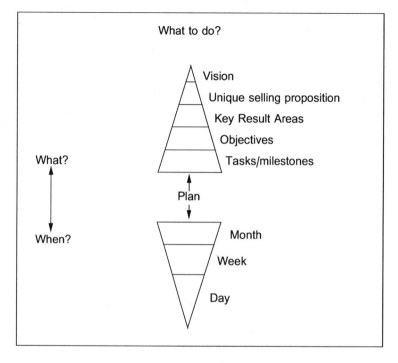

Fig. 27. Planning your activities.

PLANNING YOUR ACTIVITIES

Planning is the process by which we link what we want to achieve as a consultant (see Chapter 4 for business objectives) with when we are going to complete the critical tasks to reach our objectives. Without linking our overall business direction to our daily and weekly activities, we will not optimise our productivity (see Figure 27).

We plan for different periods of time:

- year
- quarter
- month
- week
- day.

The further away the time, the less detail there is. For example, we need very little detail on an annual plan but considerable information on a daily plan.

Weekly planning

Steven Covey in his book *First Things First* highlights the importance of weekly planning as an integral tool linking objectives and direction with weekly activities. Activities planned and prioritised weekly could include:

- contact with customers
- essential milestones from Key Result Areas
- meeting activities
- financial targets
- time with staff
- networking contacts
- marketing strategies
- new projects
- reporting activities
- percentage of time in the office/on the road
- small 'don't forget' items
- paperwork/administration.

Guidelines for planning your week

- The weekly plan is like an organised, categorised, weekly to-do list (see Figure 28).

- Plan the following week, as you are moving though the current week. When action items for the following week arise, put them on the weekly plan.

- Finalise your plan on Friday: this provides closure for the week and allows you to mentally prepare for the following week.

- Review your Key Result Areas and pick out the critical tasks that need accomplishing that week. Full details on these project milestones will be in your objectives and Key Result Areas. Don't write too much detail on your weekly plan.

- Write these milestones gathered under the Key Result Area in the two right-hand columns of your plan (see Figure 28). These tasks are not, as yet, allocated to a specific day (e.g. Xicor Proposal Team Building Programme is a task but it has no specific time allocated to it).

Task of the week: Complete Intel Leader's Guide (LG)			Week of:
Date	Schedule	KRAs	Weekly tasks/milestones
Monday	8.00 Intel design review 10.00 1.00 3.00	1. Customers ● Intel ● Oracle ● North Face ● NEC	Complete LG to design review Design team-building programme Meeting, finalise proposal Meeting
Tuesday	8.00 10.00 SGA Joe Smith 1.00 3.00	2. Prospects ● Macys ● SGA ● Frito ● Xicor	Call Meeting List of references Proposal team – building programme Follow-up call
Wednesday	8.00 10.00 1.00 Writing 3.00	3. Database 4. Finance	Add 10 new clients Invoice The North Face Monthly profit and loss
Thursday	8.00 NEC Bill Smart 10.00 North Face Mtg 1.00 3.00	5. Marketing	Draft newsletter New contracts
Friday	8.00 Team meeting 10.00 1.00 3.00	6. Administration 7. Product development	Office filing system review Prepare first draft of Making Communication Work

Fig. 28. Weekly plan – example.

Task of the week: | **Week of:** _____

Date	Schedule	KRAs	Weekly tasks/milestones
Monday	8.00 10.00 1.00 3.00		
Tuesday	8.00 10.00 1.00 3.00		
Wednesday	8.00 10.00 1.00 3.00		
Thursday	8.00 10.00 1.00 3.00		
Friday	8.00 10.00 1.00 3.00		

Fig. 29. Weekly plan – form.

136

- Write in specific appointments (e.g. North Face meeting).

- Review the best times to complete critical tasks and book time for them on your weekly plan (e.g. writing team building programme is booked on Wednesday).

It is important to select the critical milestones you need to accomplish *before* you set appointments and meetings.

Take a moment and review the example in Figure 28 and then plan next week's activities using Figure 29 if you wish. Remember, the thought process is key; the tool you use can be of your own choice.

Daily planning
Research has shown that if we have a clear picture of the next 24–48 hours, we will avoid stress and achieve more. Therefore having a clear plan of the next 24 hours can be important. Many consultants, because of the nature of their work, do not plan every day. Some only plan 'office days' because when working on a client site usually there is minimal time that is discretionary.

If you wish to plan your day, the best time to do so is the end of the previous workday. This gives you an opportunity to recognise the projects and activities completed, and allows the brain to work on the next day while you are asleep!

Many of us use 'to-do' lists, but have a problem making them work because the list tends to be a random collection of activities. Buying groceries may be in the same list as achieving a major work objective! Make sure you use your weekly plan as the source of the critical tasks for your daily plan.

A suggested approach to daily planning is as follows:

- Each day list all the activities to be completed.

- Next, assess whether any activities could be delegated, postponed or not done at all.

- With the remaining activities, assign priorities.

- Estimate time needed for each activity.

- Estimate time needed for unplanned activities such as interruptions, fire-fighting, and people demands.

- Judge whether you will need large uninterrupted blocks of time for the activities or if smaller blocks will be adequate.

Task of the day _____Date_____	
Schedule	**To Do**
6.00	_____
7.00	_____
8.00	_____
9.00	_____
10.00	_____
11.00	_____
12.00	_____
1.00	_____
2.00	_____
3.00	_____
4.00	
5.00	**Calls**
6.00	_____
7.00	_____
8.00	_____

Fig. 30. Daily plan – form.

- On a daily plan, assign a starting time to each item of work. Make sure you start on priority-one actions first.

- Match your work schedule to your body schedule.

- Don't over plan!

- Remember to build in regular breaks: the body can only concentrate for short periods of time.

Take some time now to plan tomorrow's activities, using the sample form in Figure 30.

ESTABLISHING ORGANISATION/ADMINISTRATION OBJECTIVES

You need to establish organisational objectives for your business within the administration/organisation Key Result Area. Again, these objectives need to meet the **SMART** criteria. There are normally a variety of organisational objectives for a consulting business under several categories:

- office organisation
- office equipment
- office location
- resources
- planning.

Setting clear objectives for the organisational side of your business will help ensure you make your business productive.

Now that you've seen how to organise your business, in Chapter 9 we'll finally look at actually doing the work. But first, take a moment to review the checklist, case studies and action points.

CHECKLIST

Have you:

1. Got the right equipment?

2. Set up your office?

3. Organised your paperwork filing system by Key Result Area?

4. Established current files and 'tickler files'?

5. Separated historic from current data?

6. Completed a sample weekly plan?

7. Identified a planning tool to help you in weekly planning?

CASE STUDIES

Marie works at home

Marie has decided to work at home, and has created a dedicated office space in what used to be the dining room. This is separated from the rest of the house, so she has the advantage of being able to close off the office when she is not working. She has purchased a PC clone because she believes most of her clients are on the PC platform, and she has purchased the Microsoft Office Suite™ for the same reason. While she does not have a lot of use for Excel™, she will be able to use Word™, Access™ and PowerPoint™.

She has installed two extra phone lines in her home: one for the dedicated office line, and one for the fax and e-mail. She purchased an HP printer and a combined copier/fax machine to give her some photocopying abilities, and she prefers the flexibility of a 'manual' fax machine. She has organised her filing system per Key Result Areas to tie in with her time management system, and has separated historic from current paperwork.

Having worked for a time management training company, she is used to weekly planning, and uses the form in her system for this process.

Frank gets organised

Frank has purchased a laptop computer since this will provide him with additional flexibility when he is working on long-term projects. He has also purchased a separate keyboard, screen and mouse for when he is working in the office. He prefers an electronic fax machine, because many of the documents he faxes need to be sent directly from his machine. He has begun organising his office, but has had problems separating the historic from the current data, and deciding how to store critical reference files. Since he has the space, he has converted the second bedroom in his house into an office. This is also the most cost-effective solution for him.

When planning, he refers to his contact manager from the database to remind him of key people to call and follow up with. Each week he creates a to-do list for the additional critical tasks he needs to complete within that week.

Linda rents office space

When Linda started, she believed that working from home and using her home address would not look professional, so she decided to rent office space in an executive suite. She thought this would raise the prestige of her business, plus provide a quality environment to meet with new clients. In addition, it was important to her to have a physical division between her home and office.

By renting a space she did not have to purchase a great deal of equipment or supplies, as this is provided, and she also was able to take advantage of the telephone answering services. She had begun to organise her critical files in this office space per type of service that she wishes to provide. However, now she has this three-month assignment, she doesn't need the space. Luckily she was able to sub-let the space to the person with whom she was considering a partnership.

ACTION POINTS

1. As you set up your office, furniture and equipment, think about whether a home office or separate office would fit best with your lifestyle. If you are thinking of a home office, how will you ensure the effective division between your office and work? What other office options could you consider? What equipment will be the most useful to you in running your business?

2. As you organise your office, what are the biggest challenges you face in ensuring your paperwork is easy to find and use? How will you overcome these challenges? Do you know anyone who can help you in this office organisation phase?

3. As you plan your weekly tasks and priorities, how will you ensure that you are concentrating time and energy on your Key Result Areas? How will you link the overall direction of the business to your weekly tasks? What system can you use to facilitate this process? How else will you ensure that you are focusing energy into all aspects of running your business: sales, marketing, networking, product development, finance and administration?

9

Running Your Business: Doing the Work

When you have successfully completed the key steps in setting up your consulting business as described in Chapters 2 to 8, you will be ready to actually do the work: the area in which you have the most expertise. Doing the work involves providing the functional skills and knowledge that you possess within the structure of a consulting assignment.

STRUCTURING CONSULTING ASSIGNMENTS

There are three types of consulting assignment:

1. one-off projects
2. short-term contracts
3. long-term contracts.

Ideally you want a mixture of each type of consulting assignment for your business. Each type of contract may have a mixture of the following phases:

- planning

- assessing needs

- recommending options

- implementing recommendations

- monitoring progress

- evaluating success.

The type of contract will influence the length and complexity of each assignment. The type of consulting you provide will often influence the type of contracts you receive. Marketing projects will probably be a mixture of short and long-term projects, whereas training could be a series of one-off projects.

One-off contracts

These contracts take the least planning: a simple proposal normally acts as the project plan. They normally take place in a very short time frame: one to two days. Examples could be running one training programme for a team, reviewing a service level agreement and making recommendations, editing one document, etc.

Advantages of one-off projects
- They give you a variety of activities with different clients – and greater client exposure.
- They provide you with the opportunity to 'try out' working with the client.
- They may act as a marketing possibility to obtain other work with the client.
- They give you more clients for your client list.
- They are simple to deliver and meet expectations.

Disadvantages of one-off projects
- They can take as much time to sell as a long-term contract.
- Working with many such contracts can feel like a new job every day.
- It can be hard to keep all the balls up in the air.
- They necessitate keeping contact with more people.

Short-term contracts

Short-term contracts normally have a defined beginning, middle and end, and usually range from three to ten days. Short-term contracts require slightly more planning (some of this planning can often be charged to the client) yet still remain fairly flexible in nature.

Advantages of short-term projects
- You get a variety of activities with different clients – and greater client exposure.
- It is easier to balance the workload: two or three projects at one time.
- One client does not dominate your time, thereby keeping other options open.

- You can build reasonable client relationships over a period of time.

Disadvantages of short-term projects
- If there are too many projects at one time, they can be difficult to manage.

- There is still an element of balancing multiple activities.

- If all clients want more work at one time, you may be unable to meet the demand.

- It is harder to sub-contract to others.

Long-term contracts
Long-term contracts normally have a defined beginning, middle and end, and usually last more than 15 days over a two- to three-month period, with a series of specific milestones and deliverables. These long-term contracts require more extensive planning (some of this planning can normally be charged to the client) and often need to be regularly monitored.

Advantages of long-term projects
- You focus your effort on one client so it can feel more like a 'normal job'.

- You can build a strong relationship with many contacts within one client.

- You can learn more about the company and therefore ensure that the consulting is linked to business objectives.

- You are ideally situated to continue to develop more business.

- Once you have established the payment cycle, you will normally receive regular payments.

Disadvantages of long-term projects
- If the project absorbs more than three to four days per week, marketing to other clients can suffer. A 'famine' may occur at the end of the 'feast'.

- There are often tax complications of needing to prove you are not an employee.

- If the company experiences financial difficulties your entire source of revenue can be affected.

- You may miss other opportunities because of the lack of flexibility in your schedule.

CONSULTING COMPONENTS

Planning the assignment

The time taken to plan the assignment will be directly linked to the time spent delivering the project. Increasing planning time will often increase productivity and decrease execution time.

Often the assignment is designed in the proposal stage, particularly for one-off and short-term projects. Basically you want to know who is going to do what, when, where, and how.

With long-term projects, you will need to be more specific, particularly in the early stages while credibility is being built, on deliverables and milestones. Make sure you:

- build in smaller, short-term deadlines; for example, in the design of a training project, copying the client on the initial draft of training materials

- design an initial break-through project that has a high probability of success, such as a needs assessment in the development of a training programme

- break the project into smaller do-able tasks.

Assessing needs

In most consulting assignments you need to gather all the pertinent facts or data relating to the situation. You begin the data gathering and normally determine the primary problem in the initial interview. During data gathering you must also gather information about problems which the client has not shared with you.

There are six basic data-gathering tools:

1. *Literature search.* Read any published information available.

2. *Document review.* Review all internal documentation such as operating plans and procedures, along with external documents such as financial reports from auditors, banks, etc.

3. *Interviews.* Gather information from a variety of personnel within the company, by using a structured plan, and probing on specific issues. The dynamics are very similar to the sales

interview process where you must relax the interviewee, build trust and obtain the necessary information.

4. *Questionnaires.* Distribute questionnaires both internally and externally. They can be open-ended, requiring the respondent to write in answers, or objective, where the respondents have to rate given answers.

5. *Direct observation.* Observe. Nothing can replace your own observation.

6. *Basic research.* Some projects require controlled, scientific research to collect the necessary data.

Recommending options
The information you have gathered from a variety of sources now needs to be analysed and synthesised to produce an accurate picture of the client situation. The data is analysed by reviewing any statistical data, and by using a more subjective analysis from interviews and questionnaires.

To recommend options, you have to integrate the data into a comprehensive report. During synthesis you build the pieces of data into a coherent picture. Through synthesis, the areas most in need of your and your client's attention are specified. The elements of the data are compared, prioritised and sequenced, to be combined into a meaningful whole.

The options are normally presented to the client for prioritisation and implementation planning. When developing recommendations, options can be evaluated into one or more of the following four categories:

- client must do
- client wants to do
- client can do
- client should do.

Implementing recommendations
Implementing recommendations is where the plan decided in the previous stage is delivered. Sometimes implementing the recommendations is the responsibility of the client and sometimes a consultant is used for implementation. If the client is implementing the plan, you can do several things to smooth the implementation process:

- determine who is responsible for implementation

- understand the organisational structure
- train client personnel
- monitor the new system.

If you are implementing the plan, it is critical to manage the client's expectations and keep him or her abreast of any major changes to the deliverables. Often, in the implementation stages, clients are unable to dedicate enough time and resources to the project, and as a result deadlines might slip.

Monitoring progress

Reports form an essential part of your communication with your clients. Reports may be the sole means of communicating with the client, and must contain all pertinent information relative to the progress of the project. Reports also facilitate clients' commitment to your work and give control of the project over to the consultant. There are two main types of reports:

1. *The progress report.* This documents major events, problems and solutions.

2. *The final report.* This documents the entire project, including background, methodology, findings, recommendations, and conclusions. Often the final report is the only tangible result of the project.

Major sections of the final report can include:

- table of contents
- executive summary
- project background
- objectives and scope
- methodology
- results
- findings and conclusion
- recommendations.

Evaluating project success

When you evaluate your performance both you and your client benefit. Evaluation acts as both a quality control mechanism and a learning device. Stages in evaluation are:

1. *Deciding what to evaluate* – for example:
   - customer satisfaction
   - reduced turnover
   - project outcome
   - employee morale
   - productivity.

2. *How do you evaluate?*
   - Collect pre-project data.
   - Conduct immediately after project completion.
   - Evaluate several months after project completion.
   - Select appropriate measurement tools based on the project: interviews, questionnaires, observations, etc.

3. *Documenting results*
   - Present the entire picture.
   - Document all results fully.
   - Publish to other groups.

By evaluating success you can integrate learning into new consulting assignments, and at the same time use them as a marketing tool to obtain more business.

ESTABLISHING PROJECT OBJECTIVES

You need to establish objectives for each client project. There is normally a variety of project objectives under several categories:

- customer satisfaction

- productivity increase

- number of recommendations implemented

- critical milestones

- objectives related directly to the client's needs.

Setting clear objectives for the project side of your business will help to ensure that you provide the services your clients require, which will continue to develop your business.

We have now covered from start to finish what you need to do to decide whether consulting is for you and if it is, how to start and run a successful consulting business. Read Chapter 10 for a synopsis of the steps you need to take to get into action. But first, take a moment to review the checklist, case studies and action points.

CHECKLIST

Have you:

1. Decided whether one-off, short-term or long-term projects are the best for you and your business?
2. Gathered samples of projects you completed in jobs as samples for clients?
3. Decided how you would like your work evaluated?
4. Met with other consultants who do similar work to see how they manage projects?

CASE STUDIES

Marie mixes one-off and short-term projects

Marie has decided the best plan for her business is a mix of one-off standard training programmes and short-term projects. For one-off training programmes she will work through the training broker, as this will reduce her sales and marketing time, yet still provide her with a diversity of projects. She decides to focus on time management and presentation skills standard programmes in the beginning. She has existing materials developed, plus she knows two people who could help meet client needs if she is busy when they need help. For the sales training project, she has quoted it as a short-term project with critical stages defined in the planning stage as:

- initial design
- pilot programme
- revision to class

- train trainers through the programme

- write leaders' guides

- present train-the-trainer programme for facilitators

- measure training effectiveness.

She believes this will amount to approximately 15 days of training, but will be concentrated into a month. She thinks there may be an opportunity to link the sales training programme with increases in sales. Although her initial focus was teams, in selling and marketing, these projects had the greatest short-term close rate, so she decided to do them.

With this balance of business, she thinks that she will have some solid income, but will also be able to open up doors for further training when she conducts the standard training programmes.

Frank mixes a long-term project with a short-term project
Frank has received the go ahead for the support centre re-engineering project. He has suggested two main steps for the project. The first involves conducting research into the current support centre operations, analysing current challenges and then recommending possible solutions. The second step involves working with the support centre management staff to implement the critical recommendations.

He believes phase one will go smoothly because he will be meeting with key contributors and analysing support centre operations. He is somewhat concerned about phase two, because internal personnel are extremely busy and may not have time to invest in working with him on the implementation of ideas. To this end, he wants to ensure that concrete deliverables from phase one are listed, and he has scheduled regular meetings with the vice president to keep him informed on progress.

The support centre conducts a regular customer satisfaction assessment, so he has taken ratings at the beginning of the work to act as a base line to measure possible improvements. He plans to work at this company three days a week, so he can ensure he has time to maintain his marketing efforts.

Linda works full-time as a contractor
Linda has begun working full-time as a contract financial manager and is really enjoying the assignment. She enjoys being with a team

of people, and being able to start strategies and then continue the implementation through her team. She has been given an office, computer and phone line at the company, so she is concerned about spending the money on the executive office. She is doing the assignment for three months and then will re-evaluate whether to keep the office space or not. The company is paying her on a bi-weekly basis, which is helping her concerns about money enormously. She has taken a step back from marketing, writing her business plan and meeting with networking contacts, as she has become absorbed in this position.

ACTION POINTS

1. As you consider your consulting business, to what extent will your business comprise one-off, short-term and long-term projects? How will you ensure that you capitalise on the advantages of each type of consulting work and how will you avoid any potential disadvantages?

2. As you look at each specific project, how will you ensure that you put the correct process in place to ensure the effectiveness of each contract? How will you ensure your planning is effective? What will you do to keep the client informed of progress? How will you measure the success of the project?

3. What objectives will you put in place for each project? How will you communicate these objectives to the client?

10

Moving Into Action

SO WHAT WILL YOU DO NOW?

In this book we have tried to share with you the critical steps necessary to establish your own consulting business. While many people initially are attracted to consulting, often this is because they have an unclear understanding of what it entails and the real compensation it produces.

Consulting is not a 'magic pill'. Just as with many other work opportunities, it has inherent advantages and challenges. By understanding more about consulting and yourself, it is possible to build a successful career as a consultant.

In this book:

- In Chapter 1 you were introduced to the dynamic business environment and understood why consulting is a viable and growing option for many individuals. It defined consulting, and gave parameters for the consulting industry as a whole.

- Chapter 2 described the advantages and disadvantages of consulting as a profession, and showed the critical characteristics of successful consultants. Knowing the strengths that you bring to the role of consulting and understanding potential challenges can help you succeed as a consultant.

- Chapter 3 helped you get started by defining your vision and unique selling proposition. In addition, by conducting a SWOT analysis on your potential business, you could establish Key Result Areas that exploited opportunities and minimised threats.

- Chapter 4 provided you with more detailed skills and techniques to establish your business direction by writing a clear business plan, deciding the best business structure and being specific about expectations for your business by setting objectives and milestones.

- Chapter 5 moved you from planning your strategy into business development mode, by introducing the key elements you need to market your business and the promotional strategies that will raise awareness of your services. You were encouraged to formalise your network to ensure you have the key building blocks for your business.

- Chapter 6 gave you skills and techniques in the most critical area of success for a new consultant, selling your services. Using the telephone, face-to-face meetings and proposals, you were introduced to the critical steps necessary to move the prospective client 'down the funnel' to become a paying customer.

- Chapter 7 introduced you to the critical tools for measuring your financial business success and then gave you ideas on how to ensure you charge enough for your services to make your business profitable and pay all necessary overheads.

- Chapter 8 provided ideas and techniques for organising your business for maximum effectiveness.

- Chapter 9 outlined the different types of projects and how to ensure they are successful. Finally we were able to talk about the part that most people associate with consulting – actually doing the work!

For every person who says they will never take a 'real job' again because they enjoy consulting so much, there is an another person who, having tried consulting, returns with enthusiasm to full-time work. There is no right or wrong decision: it depends on your needs and preferences.

If you follow the steps in this book and are committed to trying the process, consulting can provide you with a greater control over your own destiny and creativity, and help you to make an impact and produce results.

If you decide to return to full-time work, you still will have gained a perspective on a different lifestyle along with some skills to help you back in the workplace.

Good luck with whichever choice you make!

CHECKLIST

1. Is consulting for you?

2. Have you analysed the advantages and disadvantages of consulting objectively?

3. Have you decided your vision and established your Key Result Areas?

4. Have you defined specific, measurable, time-based, short-term objectives for yourself?

5. Have you begun to decide a marketing strategy?

6. Have you conducted some telephone calls and face-to-face meetings?

7. Have you priced your product or service competitively, yet realistically?

8. Have you got yourself organised?

9. Have you decided what type of project is the best fit?

10. Is consulting for you?

CASE STUDIES

Marie is committed to consulting

Three months after beginning consulting work, Marie has decided that she definitely wants to stay as a consultant. She enjoys being measured on the results she produces and not just her political savvy. She enjoys the variety, and despite the challenge of constant marketing, she thinks the benefits far outweigh the challenges of full-time work for her.

Frank is committed to consulting

Three months into his consulting business, Frank, to his surprise, has really enjoyed the process re-engineering project. He enjoyed working with only one client, as well as having the emotional freedom of not dealing with upset customers all the time. His networking efforts have produced a couple more interesting prospects, and so he is committed to remaining as a consultant.

Linda decides to return to full-time work

Three months into evaluating consulting as a career option, Linda has decided to return to full-time work. The organisation she is working for has offered a full-time position as an accounting manager. The organisation is small and rapidly growing. Linda believes that she will also have an opportunity to work in training as well as financial process improvements. In addition, she has enjoyed working with the team. She believes this is a better fit for her because she struggles with the marketing, and did not enjoy the 'new day/new job syndrome'. She believes the skills and techniques she picked up in the process will really benefit her in this new full-time position.

ACTION POINTS

1. Based on everything that you have read, be honest with yourself about how much you would like the constant multiplexing of projects, marketing activities and administrative tasks. What would work for you? What would be sources of stress?

2. What are the benefits to you of consulting? To what extent will the benefits outweigh the potential costs?

3. What are you going to do within the next month to make it happen, make a decision or get a new job?

Glossary

Artisan. Temperament for whom key needs are making an impact and acting on impulse.

Atomising. More and smaller businesses are performing the work that fewer and larger organisations did before.

Bad debts. Invoices issued to a client that are not paid.

Benefit. Bonus that a **feature** can provide to customers.

Break-it thinking. A methodology and training programme used to stimulate creativity and innovation in changing times.

Business plan. Four- to six-page statement of business direction, objectives and tactics.

Cash flow. Statement of cash in and cash out of the business.

Closed questions. Questions that can be answered with a 'yes' or 'no'. Used to get definitive information, or transition from one statement to another.

Consulting. Providing independent services to meet a variety of clients' needs in exchange for money.

Consulting process. Series of stages necessary to maintain a consulting business.

Contract. An agreement between two or more parties for the delivering of specified services.

Cover letter. A letter, normally accompanying a brochure, a proposal or information being sent to the client.

CV. Abbreviation of curriculum vitae, Latin for a summary of a person's educational and occupational qualifications.

Feature. Fact about your product or service.

Fractal. A pattern underlying seemingly random phenomena.

Guardian. Temperament for whom key needs are responsibility and duty/membership and belonging.

Goals. A goal is a general statement of direction.

Idealist. Temperament for whom key needs are meaning and significance/unique identity.

Key Result Areas. Your main areas of responsibility; your workload divided into categories.

Market segmentation. Dividing the market into manageable components.

Milestones. Concrete, measurable steps required to meet your **objectives**.

Mission statement. Overall statement of direction for a business showing who, and what.

Network. Database of contacts with whom you have a personal relationship, that acts as a business generation tool and a support structure.

Objectives. Concrete, tangible, measurable results or outcomes from our efforts that can be seen.

Open-ended questions. Questions that cannot be answered by a 'yes' or 'no'. Used to open up communication.

Paraphrasing. Repeating back to the client in your own words information you have gathered.

Promotional activities. Tactics outlined in the marketing plan designed to raise market awareness.

Proposal. Document used to outline a proposed approach and methodology to meet customer's needs.

Prospects. Part of your **network** that has a qualified need.

Public relations. Obtaining (unpaid) coverage in newspapers, TV, radio and magazines.

Purchase Order (PO). A statement of proposed work/costs, normally produced by the organisation, from which invoices are paid.

Rational. Temperament for whom key needs are knowledge and competence/power over destiny.

Re-engineering. The process of examining current processes and procedures and creating new approaches to improve results.

Revenue. Invoiced income.

Sales process. Steps it takes to develop business and time from start of business development to client 'booking'.

Service. Intangible advice, support, information and ideas that you provide to customers.

Situational leadership. Methodology that advocates adjusting your leadership style to the needs of your employees.

Sub-contracting. Work where there is one primary contact (the contractor) for the client. Work for other consultants is filtered through that one person.

Suspects. Part of your **network** that could generate potential business and/or act as content-knowledge experts.

SWOT analysis. The analysis of the strengths, weaknesses, opportunities and threats that face a business.

Synergy. When parts working together produce a greater result than the numerical addition of their parts i.e. $2 + 2 = 5$.

Tactician. Another name for the **artisan** temperament.

Telephone marketing. Using the telephone to obtain advice, generate appointments and get names for future business.

Temperament. Fundamental pattern of viewing the world.

Unique selling proposition. One's unique contribution within one's chosen area of expertise.

Vision statement. A picture of future greatness, a definition of core values.

Appendix:
Questions for Gathering Information

Business questions

- What is the revenue of the company?
- How many years has the company been in business?
- How many different customers does it have?
- What has been the sales growth in the past year? Two years? Etc.
- Is the company public?
- What is the financial structure of the company?
- What is the outstanding debt of the company?
- Who are the organisation's customers? Local, regional, national or international?
- Who founded the company?
- Is the founder and starter team still active in the business?
- What is the profile of the ideal customer?
- Who does what in the organisation?
- What are the main functions in the organisation?
- In the history of the company, what were the biggest advance and the biggest setback?
- What do you see as the strengths and weaknesses of this company?
- What is the highest priority in the next six months and how could you, the consultant, help?
- How is the budgeting process managed?
- In addition to revenue, what else is monitored on a regular basis?
- What is the most profitable line of business and what are the development plans for this line?

- What is the company's compensation philosophy?
- What is the company's training philosophy?

Culture questions

- What does the company have written about its culture? In terms of annual reports, quarterly statement, brochures?
- Can all individuals state the company's mission or reason for being? Do individuals have a clear picture of its values?
- What are the slogans in the organisation?
- How do beliefs affect the day-to-day business of the organisation?
- What are the stories in the organisation?
- What is the physical environment? How does it compare to the settings for the social styles? What evidence does it give of the type of culture?
- What are the rites and rituals present in the organisation? How are high performers recognised? What are the opportunities for team recognition? What are the team activities supported by the company?
- How are meetings managed? (If possible, try and attend a meeting.) How often are meetings held? For the team? For individuals? How do employees get involved in meetings? Where do people sit?
- How are new employees hired and introduced to the company?
- What awards are given in the organisation? What values do these awards reinforce?
- Are there language rituals, such as the extensive use of jargon? How are individuals addressed?
- What are the unwritten rules of behaviour in the organisation? e.g. Nepotism? Sexist jokes? Dress code?
- Are there predefined standards for presentation of materials?
- How and when are memos used in the organisation?
- Who are the heroes of the organisation? Why are they recognised as such? What does this demonstrate about the culture?

- What are people like who work at the organisation? How long have they been there?

- What is the staff turnover rate?

- How do you feel about the president or CEO? What do you recognise about his or her social style?

- How are strangers greeted in the organisation?

- What is the format of the average day?

- What is the company's strategic planning process?

- What are the main communication channels? Formal or informal?

- How do these communication channels work?

- How are decisions made in the company? Is there a formal chain of command for decisions? How far does the president delegate decision-making?

Market questions

- What market segment is the organisation part of?

- How is the industry structured?

- What is the organisation's role in the way the industry is structured?

- What is unique about the way the company competes?

- Who are the company's major competitors?

- What is the company's specific market niche?

- What promotional strategies are used within this market niche?

- What is the industry outlook?

- What are the plans to expand to new market areas?

Current environment questions

- What current challenges are facing the business?

- What is being done to address the challenges?

- What changes have taken place in the past few months?

Further Reading

BUSINESS INFORMATION

The Age of Unreason, Charles Handy, Harvard Business School Press, 1991

Consulting, Robert E. Kelly, Scribner, 1986

If It Ain't Broke, Break It, Robert J. Kriegel and Louis Patter, Warner Books, 1992

Management of Organizational Behavior, Paul Hersey, et al, Prentice Hall, 1996

New Venture Creation, Jeffry A. Timmons, Richard d Irwin, 1994

Up Your Own Organization, Donald M. Dible, Out of Print

SELF-ASSESSMENT

Do What You Are, Paul D. Tieger and Barbara Barron-Tieger, Little Brown & Co., 1995

Please Understand Me, David Keirsey and Marilyn Bates, Prometheus Nemesis Book Co., 1984

Please Understand Me II, David Keirsey and Stephen Montgomery, Prometheus Nemesis Book Co., 1998

Beside Ourselves, Naomi L. Quenk, Consulting Psycholgists Press, 1994

SELF IMPROVEMENT

How to Get Control of Your Time and Your Life, Alan Lakein, New American Library, 1996

First Things First, Steven Covey, et al, Fireside, 1996

Index

administration, 23, 26, 43–45, 50, 134–135, 139, 141
advertising, 70–74, 79, 106
artisan, 24, 34, 93, 156, 158
atomising, 12, 13, 156

bad debts, 114, 120, 123–124, 156
benefits, 26, 29–30, 50, 53, 62, 66–69, 72, 74, 76, 86, 93–94, 96–98, 102, 113, 115, 124, 154–155
billing rate, 112–116, 123
business cards, 32, 74, 76, 80, 94, 106, 130
business development, 25, 44, 46, 50, 56, 64, 72, 75, 81, 86, 104–105, 107, 152, 157
business plan, 42–43, 46, 48–49, 51, 54, 58–62, 108, 110, 130, 151–152, 156

cash flow statements, 49, 110, 112
capital, 18, 23, 31, 35–36, 38, 62, 107–108, 124, 151
clients, 13, 15–16, 19, 22–24, 27, 29, 44, 49–50, 56, 58, 61, 68–71, 73–75, 77–78, 81–82, 84–86, 93, 99, 102–103, 105, 112, 114–115, 117–118, 120, 122, 124, 126–132, 135, 140–141, 143–144, 147, 149, 156

closed questions, 156
collecting fees, 119
consulting assignments, 142, 145, 148
consulting process, 21, 27–31, 70, 156
contracts, 101, 122, 124, 131, 135, 142–144
costs, 12, 50, 53, 74, 79, 86, 106–107, 110–114, 123, 126, 129, 155, 157
cover letters, 74–75, 101
credibility, 24–25, 27–29, 73–74, 79, 88, 145

database, 44, 55–56, 59, 61–62, 65–66, 75–78, 80, 83, 102, 104, 129, 135, 141, 157

e-mail, 76, 78–80, 104, 128, 130, 140
equipment, 16, 56, 106, 110, 112, 124, 128, 139, 141
ethics, 25, 27–29
evaluation, 23, 86, 148
exhibitions, 70, 72, 76

features, 66–69, 74, 93, 96–98
fees, 52, 99, 113, 116–120
fee structures, 119, 125
financial objectives, 109, 123, 125

goals, 26, 33–34, 39–41, 50, 54, 61–52, 156

idealist, 24, 29, 33, 94, 156

key clients, 77
Key Result Areas, 32, 34, 39–48, 54–59, 61, 63, 132, 134, 140–141, 152, 154, 156

legal structure, 51, 54, 58, 59
limited company, 52–53
listening, 22, 95–97, 105
long-term contracts, 142, 144

mailings, 70, 75, 82
market research, 42, 46, 49, 63–65, 69–70, 72, 77–78, 80
market segmentation, 157
marketing, 14–17, 19, 22–25, 29–30, 34, 37–38, 41–42, 44–46, 49–50, 59, 61–63, 65–66, 68–70, 72, 75, 77–78, 80–83, 86–87, 103, 107, 110, 115, 123, 128, 130, 134–135, 141–144, 148–151, 154–155
marketing communications, 70, 74
marketing plan, 49, 63, 66, 69, 71, 78, 80, 157
milestones, 39, 40, 48, 51, 54–55, 58–62, 99, 116, 120, 132, 134–137, 144–145, 148, 152, 157
mission statement, 34, 157

needs assessment, 104, 142, 145
network, 25–30, 33, 38, 42, 45–46, 63, 65, 72, 75–77, 80, 83–86, 89, 104–105, 107, 125, 131, 134, 141, 151, 153–154, 157
newsletters, 55–56, 59, 66, 70, 72, 75, 77

objectives, 8, 33, 39, 48, 51, 54–66, 70, 77–78, 80, 85, 95, 97, 99, 109, 110, 139, 144, 147–148, 151–152, 154, 156–157
office space, 16, 126–127, 140–141, 151
one-off projects, 142–143
open-ended questions, 93, 95, 97–98, 105, 157
operations, 14, 41, 45, 51, 90, 113, 150
organisation (of paper), 23, 58, 131–132, 134, 140, 141
overhead expenses, 113

paraphrasing, 96–97, 103, 157
partnership, 51–53, 62, 78, 141
planning, 14, 24, 26, 32, 40, 48, 50–51, 78, 80, 85, 88, 104, 126, 133–134, 137, 139–146, 149, 151–152, 161
product development/definition, 12, 44–46, 50, 56, 135, 141
profit, 34, 48–49, 51, 53, 66, 106–109, 111–115, 135, 153, 159
projects, 18–19, 23, 25, 29–30, 39, 41, 45, 50, 58, 60, 85, 99–100, 113, 117, 123, 131, 134, 137, 140, 142–146, 149–151, 153–155
promotional activities, 71, 78, 157
proposals, 22, 75, 84–86, 97, 99, 103, 105, 153
prospects, 22, 45, 55–56, 61, 73, 76–77, 79, 83–86, 92, 102–105, 129, 135, 154, 157
public relations, 70, 73–74, 157

rational, 24, 30, 33, 94, 157
retainer, 117–118
revenue, 17, 22, 29, 53, 55, 71, 77, 109–113, 115, 122–125, 129, 131, 144, 157, 159

sales meeting, 93–94, 96–98
sales process, 82, 84–85, 97, 105, 157
selling skills, 33, 35–37, 39, 43, 45–49, 61, 65, 69, 81–82, 84–86, 88–89, 95–97, 102, 153, 158
Shamrock organisation, 8, 12
short-term contracts, 142–143
skills, 12–13, 17, 22–23, 25, 27–31, 33, 35, 38, 45, 82, 84, 93, 96–98, 105, 113, 149, 152–153, 155
sole proprietor, 51
speeches, 69–70, 73
start up costs, 106–107, 123
stationery, 16, 106, 129–130

sub-contracting, 121–123, 157
suspects, 56, 77, 83, 85–86, 102, 104–105, 119, 157
SWOT analysis, 37–39, 43, 45, 47–49, 61, 152, 157

telephone marketing, 81, 86–87, 103, 158
temperament, 23–24, 33, 93, 156–158
trade shows, 72

unique selling proposition, 32, 35–37, 39, 43, 45–49, 61, 65, 88–89, 152, 158

vision statement, 33–35, 43, 45–46, 49, 158

web, 12, 66, 70, 72–73, 78–79, 128
web pages, 72

MANAGING YOUR BUSINESS ACCOUNTS
How to keep the books and maintain financial control over your business

Peter Taylor

Now in its fifth edition and updated to take account of recent changes in the law, students as well as business managers will find this book refreshingly simple and easy to use. 'It will help you to sort out the best way to carry out double entry book-keeping, as well as providing a clear step-by-step guide to accounting procedures.' *Mind Your Own Business*. 'Takes one through the basic steps in simple language.' *Western Morning News*. 'Compulsory reading both for those starting a new business and those already in the early stages.' Manager, National Westminster Bank (Midlands). Peter Taylor is a Fellow of the Institute of Chartered Accountants. He has many years' practical experience of advising small businesses, especially on taxation and auditing matters.

184pp. illus. 1 85703 536 4. 5th edition.

MASTERING BOOK-KEEPING
A complete step-by-step guide to the principles of accounting

Peter Marshall

Illustrated at every stage with specimen entries, the book will be an ideal companion for students taking LCCI, RSA, BTEC, accountancy technician and similar courses at schools, colleges or training centres. Typical business transactions are used to illustrate all the essential theory, practice and skills required to be effective in a real business setting. 'An interesting approach.' *Association of Business Executives Journal*. 'A complete step-by-step guide...each section of the book teaches a useful skill in its own right.' *OwnBase*. 'In addition to providing a useful approach to the teaching and learning of book-keeping skills, the way in which the text is presented should ensure that the book also provides a valuable reference source for revision and prompting.' *Teeline*.

192pp. illus. 1 85703 495 3. 4th edition.

STARTING YOUR OWN BUSINESS
How to plan and build a successful enterprise

Jim Green

Now in its second edition, this dynamic guide explores the vital steps to creating a business. It shows you how to conceptualise, set up and operate any small business successfully, from preparing a business plan and launching the venture, to developing marketing strategies and selling techniques. 'Practical advice presented in a clear and concise style.' *Moneywise*. 'An easy-to-read and motivating book.' *Making Money*. Jim Green writes and lectures on business topics.

160pp. illus. 1 85703 274 8. 2nd edition

SETTING UP A LIMITED COMPANY
How to form and operate a company as a director and shareholder

Robert Browning

Limited liability represents a responsibility to the general public and gives business dealings a public face. Directors, too, have onerous responsibilities. This book has been written by Robert Browning, a chartered accountant formerly in public practice with many years' experience of small businesses. It sets out simply how to decide whether a company is right for you and, if so, how to go about it. Apart from a detailed explanation of how to form a company, it covers the filing of statutory information, the opening of bank accounts, taxation, wages and salaries, marketing, auditing and accountancy, and the use of computers.

136pp. illus. 1 85703 452 X. 2nd edition.

COPING WITH SELF ASSESSMENT
How to complete your tax return and minimise your tax bill

John Whiteley

'If you dare to do your own tax return, this book needs to be on your bookshelf'. Laurel Alexander, *Working From Home.* Save time and money with this step-by-step-guide. It takes you through everything from completing the forms correctly to surviving an Inland Revenue enquiry. What do you do if you make an error in your claim and how do you make payments on account? The answers are all here, together with ways to avoid penalties, interest and surcharges, plus a chapter on paying less tax. John Whiteley is a Chartered Accountant who has successfully advised taxpayers from all walks of life.

160pp. illus. 1 85703 580 1. 4th edition.

MAKING DIRECT MAIL WORK
Get great results from all your direct mail

Peter Arnold

Direct Mail is a proven and effective method of promotion for almost every type of organisation, large or small. Love it, or hate it, direct mail works. Any small company, or even self-employed people, can take advantage of this most flexible and controllable of all promotional media. This book sets out, in a simple and graphic way, exactly how to initiate and run your own direct mail system. It also shows you how to avoid the pitfalls and maximise effectiveness and efficiency. Peter Arnold has been creating and writing direct mail campaigns for over 35 years, and is one of the most experienced professionals in Britain. He has worked for every sort of organisation from the large multinational to the one and two-man operation.

120pp. illus. 1 85703 297 7.